Get Your Head Out of Your Asana

- The Yoga Book That Isn't -

Jason Revere

with Sandra Guy

Get Your Head Out of Your Asana
- The Yoga Book That Isn't -

-

978-90-829011-0-8
You Can Yoga

Copyright © Jason Revere 2018

Jason Revere has asserted his right under the Copyright, Designs and Patents Act 1988 to be identified as the author of this work.

-

Photography by Rolf Eijtjes
Cover design by Demian Rosenblatt

-

All rights reserved

Contents

"Nothing is true. Everything is permitted."
- *Ron Swanson, city official*

Now, why am I here?

"There is no 'I' in self."
- *Jason Revere, yogi*

I am here as a result of my own awakening. This book documents that process, as it has happened - and as it is continuing to happen - inside me.

What led me here was my own personal yoga practice and a lifetime of questioning. When I arrived, it surprised me that no one had told me exactly what the awakening process would be like. If someone *had* tried to tell me, they failed. Or, more likely, I wasn't ready or listening. I was shocked that I had spent so many years on assorted spiritual paths only to end up in a place I had never heard of or, better yet, never been warned about.

As funny as it sounds, now I'm awake and have no emotional attachment to my past; but I still feel the need to share this story in the hope that it will guide others. Keep in mind as you journey with me that all of this is new and I'm still trying to navigate reality as I now see it.

I'm also here to tell you that being awake is nothing like you think it will be.

The spiritual marketplace is more like a midnight bazaar. It's filled with tantalizing variations on the same theme – none of which are completely true, at least not outside of Maya. (Maya is the collective reality in which we all think we live.) Each dish only delivers a small part of the whole. That midnight bazaar is a place of chaos and delight and, if you pile it all together, it's very easy to get lost. Maya's spell of illusion is well woven and strong. My goal is to help you break free from it.

The only real truth is the one you already know but aren't completely aware of. The one that sits deep within you that you always find a way to drown out or avoid. We have to actively uncover, release and awaken it.

All my years of study and practice have led me to two simple facts: I know nothing and I do not exist.

Beyond that lies the real truth. The answer to all of life's questions.

Consciousness.

The True Self.

I want to give you a glimpse of what living this way might mean and then show you how to find it.

I write this book with the same intention I had when I opened my first yoga school in Amsterdam in 2012. This was something I needed access to in my life, but it didn't exist. So I needed to create something that allowed me to move forward in my own evolution - and this was it. With this book I want to show you how simple it can be to wake up from the dream we call life; to take control, awaken to your True Self and redesign the way you live to embrace your fullest potential.

That said, just because it's simple doesn't mean it's fast or easy. Though this is a basic approach to life, the work is long and arduous, and the process as challenging as it is intense. I am only a guide; you have to be ready and willing to do the work yourself.

Helpful things to know

"God is not anything human.
God is a force, God is chaos, God is unknown.
God is terror and enlightenment at the same time."
- *Ralph Fiennes, actor*

For the purpose of this book, I'd like to share some basic language that's helpful to know when we talk about waking up and enlightenment. If you've been on a yoga/spiritual journey for a while, feel free to give this section a pass.

Asana - The physical postures that are performed during a yoga class.

Atman - In Sanskrit it means "self." This is the little piece of Brahman / Consciousness of which you are made. The True Self.

Awake - Knowing that there is something bigger going on around you. Seeing what we know to be, is, in fact, questionable. Knowing your place in the world. Awareness of Atman.

Brahman - In the Hindu religion this refers to Consciousness, The Supreme Cosmic Spirit, the absolute, all that there is. God, if you will. Everything.

Conscious Creation - Once awake, we can influence our lives by following the cues and signs given by the universe and acting upon them. Thus we can consciously create the life we want.

Ego/Self - You as you *think* you are. The self that you relate to. The you that feels emotions, that lives your life for you. The character.

Enlightenment - Death of the self. No longer living within the illusion of Maya.

False Reality - The world as we know it. Everything that we think is real. False Reality is projected onto the screen of Maya.

Maya - The veil or "illusion" in Sanskrit, the screen onto which the movie of your life is projected. Everything that makes up you and your connection to the False Reality.

Yoga - The practice of quieting the mind in order to confront the ego so that you can separate yourself from it and experience Atman.

Yoga Bubble - The space within Maya that yogis tend to create and get lost in. The coddling of the ego within the warm embrace and safety of spiritual teachings and beliefs.

Yogi - A person who has decided to seek the truth.

Why are you here?

"I shall no longer be instructed by the Yoga Veda or
the Aharva Veda, or the ascetics, or any other doctrine
whatsoever. I shall learn from myself, be a pupil of myself;
I shall get to know myself, the mystery of Siddhartha."
He looked around as if he were seeing the world
for the first time.
- *Herman Hesse, Siddhartha*

Sandra and I sit down to a light lunch in the lounge at
the studio to discuss what it means to be truly awake. She is
our resident acupuncturist, also my own, and it recently came
up in one of our sessions. We discuss many things as I lie on
her treatment table covered in needles. That day I was telling
her about experiences I have had in my awakening process
and how I use those experiences in my work with my
students. The first question I always ask them is, *Why are
you here?*

"So," Sandra says between mouthfuls of her sandwich, "If we go back to the idea of writing a book, I'd probably start by asking you that very question. Why are you here today?"

"Me, myself?"

"Yes. You, yourself."

I think for a moment. "In what sense? My False Self or my True Self?"

"Both." She laughs. "The whole orange. I want the whole story."

We'll come back to oranges later. Right now, I'm thinking about who is sitting here answering her questions, and why.

"The False Self is here as a yoga teacher," I say. "But also as a sort of awakening person who has this desire to share the process with other people because it was nothing like I ever imagined it would be. Nothing in all the books I'd read, all the yoga I'd practiced and all the studying I'd done over my entire life prepared me for the process as it happened."

"So what did you imagine? What were you thinking it would be like?" she asks.

"Well, you know, the usual. You think it's like Bliss, Nirvana, the sort of stereotypical ideas that usually count as Enlightenment.

"Let me give you an example. About fifteen years ago, I was doing an advanced teacher training course in the mountains in Northern California. We were studying *The*

Upanishads and *Vedas*, the ancient philosophical texts of Hinduism, and the philosophy was having a profound effect on how I was thinking about yoga as a whole. After a day of particularly intense study, I found myself under a large oak tree near the forest that had a swing attached to one of the lower branches. I sat myself down to watch the sunset and while I was there, gently swinging back and forth absorbing the day's content, I had a moment of total understanding, total union with the world and all things around me. In that instant everything made sense. And with this understanding came a calmness, a silence in my mind and an openness in my heart. It was as if my heart was on fire. As if it had turned into a massive ball of energy that was opening up and connecting with the universe around me. I, as a separate individual, began to dissolve and as I did, I understood the concept of union – at least how it had been taught to me – for the first time. As if in celebration of that realization, a small herd of eight deer came out of the woods and grazed around me until darkness settled.

"I thought I had arrived. That this was Enlightenment. But that moment was fleeting and though it was magical and mystical, it was not Enlightenment. Enlightenment is painful and permanent. This was beautiful and, yes, it was something, but Enlightenment it was not.

"Connection is certainly a part of Enlightenment but it's only a small part because once you wake up, you don't actually care about all the little things that concerned you so much before – and that's completely liberating.

"But the point is, I want people to understand that nothing they do can really prepare them for where they are going on this path. And if they keep looking outside of themselves for the answer, they will never find it."

Sandra glances at the many books stacked atop shelves in the studio, an eyebrow raised.

I continued. "Of course, I've read plenty of spiritual books. I've studied many religions. I've done yoga for over twenty years and I've practiced with many teachers – but very few who were truly awake. The thing that helped me really progress was when I stopped reading books and stopped looking for new teachers. It was the moment I looked inside and started using my own thought process to tear apart what I believed was true and what I believed was not."

Sandra's still looking wistfully at the books. She's not convinced by my argument. "And what made you stop looking outside? What was the process of actually stopping, because you were actively searching and then suddenly you stopped? Why?"

I try to remember. "There were steps along the way. It's like I would get excited by one thing and then realize it was giving me nothing back. Like I had exhausted that particular avenue of information. I'd read the *Bhagavad Gita* and I felt like, *OK, that's a nice story.* I got the fundamental baseline, the point they were trying to make. It made sense rationally but it didn't have an effect on my consciousness or my awareness. None at all. I understood the principal of the story, and what I was supposed to take from it was clear, but reading the book didn't make it happen. Does that make sense?"

She frowns. "The book showed you what to expect but didn't help make it happen?"

"Didn't make it happen at all. It was just a nice story with a nice message. Showing me what was possible. But it didn't give a roadmap on how to get there."

"The book was like a window, then, to see where you might like to go? But it gave no instructions on how to open that window or crawl out?"

"Exactly."

"So you started with yoga? Was that your first step in wanting to know what was out there?"

I laugh. "No, my first step was in a totally different direction. I was raised in a divorced family. One side was Protestant and the other was Catholic. One weekend I was Protestant and the next weekend I was Catholic. Back and forth from parent to parent, from one church to another. Of course, it makes you ask questions because you are seeing two completely different religions that are based on the same text from the Bible. And that makes you question the value of a text. How can a text be so heavily interpreted that one version of it contradicts another?

"I started to ask questions because I wanted to know the truth. I was very young and the church members in both churches couldn't answer my questions. When I saw one thing at one church that contradicted something from the other, I would be vocal about it. And when they couldn't answer me, I thought, *If you can't answer the questions of a child, I can't trust you. I can't take you seriously.* After that I spoke to my mother. I told her that going to Church wasn't bringing me anything, so I wanted out. She allowed me to stop.

"But I continued to explore the Bible because at the time it was all I knew about spirituality. So I read the whole thing. Twice! And there, too, I thought *good story.* I didn't see how it could have created all of this religious chaos in the world because the interpretations were so varied. That's when I remember thinking for the first time that this book isn't real. The purpose of this story, whether it was intended to be an awakening process or not, wasn't working. At least, not anymore.

After that I started exploring other things, nature based religions like Druidism, Wicca, Paganism, Witchcraft. I wanted to focus on ideas based on the earth and elements."

"The natural world."

"Exactly. Something that you could put your hands on. But, of course, that's not real either!"

"But I still wanted something that was tangible. You know what I mean? I went on to discover all of this voodoo stuff from my grandma – she was a witch in Louisiana and believed in these things. And, again, I thought I was touching something real. That I had learned something but my awareness or my consciousness didn't actually change. I thought, *OK, that's not what I wanted, either. Sure, you can connect to the elements, the earth and the seasons but that's all a construct, too. A kind of reality we've agreed on. Maya.*

"I still had questions, so I shifted to Eastern philosophy. Same story. I wanted something to change my perspective of reality and give me some truth. But, it did not."

Sandra's looking puzzled, again. "There must have been a gauge that you were using for the truth. Something specific you were seeking because it wasn't only an intellectual understanding. And it wasn't about connecting to a larger force in yourself because you would have gotten that with nature, the sun or the moon."

"Do you think?" I ask. In my mind a connection to nature, the sun and the moon are still only constructs of Maya. I always felt there had to be something bigger than that.

"What do you think you were searching for?" Sandra asks. "You say now, as an adult, that it didn't change your perception or awareness but as a child, as a younger person, you must have been driven by something more than wanting to change your awareness. It must have been something you were hungry for, or thirsty for, that you wanted to touch, or wanted to know or even needed to know, because otherwise you would have gotten distracted."

"I think the answer that most people want when they are seekers or are on a personal spiritual quest is the very basic: "Why?"

"Why?" Sandra repeats.

"Why are you here?" I chuckle. We had previously played with that as the title for this book and it's still relevant.

She smiles. "There we go. Was that your first question? *Why am I here? Or why did something happen?*"

"I never questioned why things happened. I always accepted that things just happen. Not like when you go through puberty and think, *Why me, why me?* It wasn't that. It was bigger than that. It was more, *So what's the fucking point?*"

"And what *was* the point? Was it the search for meaning itself? Or finding something that meant something for you?"

"I suppose I was searching for some sort of meaning to existence. I thought, *Okay, we are here, this is cool, but what's actually going on?*"

"So you had an innate sense that there was something else going on that was separate from what you experienced?"

"I always had the feeling that something was going on that I didn't understand. I'm very inquisitive, though. Everything I do, I question. *Why is it like this? What makes this work?*"

"A hands on approach to metaphysics, in fact?"

I laugh. "If you could put your hands on those sorts of things, I guess."

"So, if we go back to my original question, *Why are you here?*, you chose to answer it from your False Self as the yoga teacher looking for meaning."

"Yes, that person is always looking for that answer."

"But what about your True Self? What is your True Self and what is he/she/it doing sitting here answering my questions?"

"The True Self doesn't care one way or another because the True Self isn't attached to those concepts or ideas. The True Self is basically your small portion of Brahman. This is where talking about the Hindu concepts of Brahman, Atman and Maya are relevant.

"In this case, Brahman would be consciousness. Consciousness, as we know it, is the only thing that is real. It's the only thing that exists.

"Atman is your piece of consciousness – the bit of consciousness that makes you who you are, and it's temporary because your physical body is here and the consciousness you experience everything through while being in this body is Atman. Atman is only a small piece of Brahman. Basically we are here for the education and entertainment of Brahman."

"Education?" Sandra asks. "As in educating yourself?"

"Not in the sense of you actually learning something, but for the sake of consciousness in general. We are all experiencing something completely different. Every single person's life is completely different from that of another but all that experience, all that consciousness goes back to the same source. It's all an experience for Brahman."

"And Maya?"

"Maya would be everything else."

Sandra looks puzzled. "Okay..."

"That's a bit much for a first chapter though. . ."

So, you walk into a bar with Brahman and Maya.
The barmaid asks, "What will it be?"
Brahman replies, "I'm good, I'm everything."
You say, "I'll have what he's having!"
Maya laughs, "Uhmm, no. No, you won't."

That little piece of air
is suffocating

"For a seed to achieve its greatest expression,
it must come completely undone. The shell cracks,
its insides come out and everything changes.
To someone who doesn't understand growth,
it would look like complete destruction."
- *Cynthia Occelli, author*

Sandra and I continue our discussion on the nature of reality. "I'm interested in this idea of oranges and the nature of truth," she says. "Remember we started talking about truth and the anatomy of oranges?"

"Oh, yes, that little bit of air inside."

Sandra gestures out the window to the studio courtyard. "You said everything out there is Maya. So to find the truth you have to go within because what's inside is more real than what's out there."

I nod.

"Yet in Western culture, in general, what's on the inside is what's considered subjective, not real. What's real is what is on the outside - seen and agreed upon by everyone."

"Of course, because as people we only associate with Maya in general."

Sandra sighs. "It would be great to have some sort of image, like the orange, to represent that, you know, peeling a fruit until the inside becomes the outside."

"You mean a visual to show the process more clearly?"

"Yes, like the image of a lotus flower growing out of the mud. The idea that you can bloom, even in difficult circumstances. But what we need here is a different image, and I'm not sure what we could use. Maybe something like a whirlwind or whirlpool to show that you are the still point at the center and everything turning around you is Maya and beyond that is only more Maya. Or something..."

"Well, imagine if the process of awakening were an orange. You would peel off the pieces of the False Self – the skin first, and then the segments of fruit. If it were an onion you would take each false layer and rip it away, one by one, as well."

"And the essential truth?" Sandra asks, "The essential truth would be?"

"What's in the middle. What's left when all those other layers are gone."

"If you take an orange apart, what are you left with? Seeds?"

"No." I grin. "In the center of an orange is a small pocket of air – an empty space."

"So, maybe, that's it? The image to clarify the process? Because you aren't just talking about the peel. You're not talking about the fruit. You're not even talking about the seeds at the center. You're talking about getting to that empty space at the heart of the fruit inside."

"Yes. Peel back an orange, the exterior could represent Maya. The pieces of flesh and even the seeds could represent your physical and emotional connections to Maya and all that's left when you get rid of those things is your True Self – a little piece of air. And that little piece of air is suffocating!"

Selective vacations

"It's paradoxical, yet true, to say that the more we know, the more ignorant we become in the absolute sense, for it is only through enlightenment that we become conscious of our limitations. Precisely one of the most gratifying results of intellectual evolution is the continuous opening up of new and greater prospects."
- *Nikola Tesla, physicist*

Sandra and I are back in the studio contemplating oranges. She's turning a small one over in her hand, staring at it. "So, you're saying the True Self lies in the space at the center of an orange? That's a very clear image."

I feel a "but" coming on.

"But the image you used when you talked about Brahman and Atman was the ocean. Where is the True Self in the ocean?"

"I used the ocean as a representation of consciousness – to give you a visual. Think about the ocean. If you take a glass and fill it, you have a small piece of the ocean. It has its own identity and responds and acts differently than the ocean but it's still just the ocean. If the glass breaks, the water simply goes back to being ocean."

"What's the difference then between that glass of ocean and rain going into a river and then into the ocean?"

"The rain came from the ocean. It's evaporated consciousness. It's going to have its personal experience and then return back to the source."

"And there's no point in that for you? There's no higher meaning to the collection of that personal experience."

"I don't know, I'm not Brahman."

"Yet. Your consciousness has not returned to its source – yet."

We laugh.

"I'm very self aware. Aware of my Atman, my True Self. I guess I've always somehow been that way. Why? Who knows? Maybe when all you are is consciousness there isn't much else to do? I only know where I fit in, and that's it. Me as Atman. I also know that what I thought of as reality is no longer my reality."

"How did that happen? We talked about this movement through Christianity, through the nature religions, through Eastern and Middle Eastern philosophical teachings, and then what happened?"

"I got angry because none of it made any sense and nothing took me anywhere different. I always felt like I ended up in the same place and I really got angry. Furious, even. I had this fire burning inside of me like *Why the fuck does nothing actually make sense?* Because nothing made any sense to me. Nothing at all.

"It was anger about that which drove my focus and my intent. As much as people might want to think that meditation, chanting, yoga and religious study will bring them to some point of awakening, it won't. It just puts you deeper into your own personalized Maya distraction. Instead of getting your head out of the sand you're burying yourself deeper in it.

"Nothing I read or studied gave me a sense that I was actually developing consciously. I was learning things that I didn't know how to apply to my life. But the anger really made me focus my thought process on trying to understand what I was feeling. And it was something like – *If all of this shit has been around for centuries, where are the results? Why are people still fucked? Why are we still killing each other, fighting each other, living for consumerism and all these false things?*

"None of the traditions I studied had answers to those

questions and that made them irrelevant. None of them were real. None were true.

The awakening process is basically truth Awareness. You become aware that no religion has all the answers. Not one of them is true."

"Not even collectively – i n a new agey approach you can have a bit of Buddhism here, a bit of something else thrown in there?"

I groan. "That's even worse. Nothing quite works so you make up your own by cherry picking. When you do that you're creating a bubble of things that make you feel better, that give you peace of mind. And that bubble doesn't wake you up, it enslaves you. And if you are enslaved, you are trapped."

"There is an interesting dichotomy coming up here between a sense of awakening and a sense of peace."

I nod. "They are two completely separate things."

"And what you are suggesting is that some of the practices thought to help awaken you, like a strong meditation practice, actually ensconce you deeper in Maya. Meditation can bring a lot of peace but that's completely different from an awakening?"

"Peace of mind and awakening are two completely different things. That's why the question I first ask my coaching clients is *Why are you here?* I'm actually asking *What do you want? Do you just want peace of mind? Cool. I can teach you all the stuff my False Self learned to placate it and when you learn how to do it for yourself, it will give you a very peaceful life. And if that's what you want, that's fine."*

"To a lot of people, a peaceful life is an aspiration." Sandra sighs. "There is a lot of mindfulness training these days which focuses on peace of mind, and when people go through a lot of turmoil what they search for, fundamentally, is a sense of peace because in peace you can restore your self, your health and your vision of who you are and where you want to go."

I smile. "But that's still within the reality of the False Self."

"So there is peace, and that can be a very constructive way of operating within this world as it stands?"

"Yes, but that's not awakening. That's just creating a space in False Reality, in Maya, that works for you. A space that keeps your life smooth and simple. You get a better understanding as to how things work but you haven't really crossed the border into True Reality. You know what I mean?"

"And crossing the border is crossing into awakening?"

"It's starting to recognize Maya for what she really is."

"Which is?"

"Everything around you. Everything that you think is real. It's all Maya, and it's all distraction – usually through your emotions. War, peace, love – all of these things that have an emotional charge stop you from thinking for yourself. They are all Maya."

"So, if I'm right, you are saying an emotional

connection to something creates a greater distance between you and a world without Maya?"

"Emotion pulls you deeper into Maya. That's all."

"If we think about some of the things you are saying from a fictional point of view you would have some evil power keeping this whole race enchained in some kind of slumber."

"That's exactly what Maya is, but she, it, is not an evil power. It's just what we have created. It's what Maya does and what Maya is. It's a self-created illusion. We say things are true when they are not."

Sandra looks a little sad. "Do you still feel joy at seeing a beautiful sunset or a golden field of barley, or the stars?"

"I love watching life go by. I love watching it completely, and it's beautiful. It's even more beautiful because I know it's not real and it's temporary. It's like a vacation."

"A selective vacation."

"Because there are no high ups and downs anymore. Everything is moving on a nice smooth plateau."

"Which you could say is a state of peace."

"Total peace."

Sandra frowns. "I thought you said that awakening and peace are not the same thing. That they are almost opposites. . ."

"Well, you can meditate for 20 years and do yoga and come out exactly the same as when you began. You might be a very peaceful person but you are not necessarily one who is awake."

"But isn't peace a requisite to deciding to awaken?" She gnaws on her nail, thinking. "I mean, life can be pretty chaotic. Finding peace through a disciplinary practice like meditation might be a first step in deciding what comes next. So out of a state of peace you can choose to awaken?"

"Well, you can choose to keep going but you can also choose to be peaceful within the state of Maya, that's fine. Nothing changes in the way you see the world. Nothing really changes in the way you behave in that world – except that you are able to find peace in what you know. You still know nothing."

"So in an ideal evolution, if there is such a thing, or an evolution into awakening you might go from that state of good practice, peaceful detachment and mindfulness into choosing to awaken. And at that moment everything would shift."

I cock my head, thinking. "No, awakening isn't about simple shifts. Otherwise everyone would be awake. You awaken by attacking everything you know. You don't awaken by going deeper into your spiritual practice. You awaken by going farther away from it."

"So it's like reaching a tipping point and choosing for change or something . . ."

I shake my head. "Not exactly. There is no tipping point in spiritual practice. There isn't one because you could go live on an ashram your whole life and go deeper into Hinduism or yogic philosophy but that doesn't mean you are any more awake. You're just buried deeper in that segment of Maya. I used to read as much as I could and piled up as much information and philosophy inside of me as possible. I guess I was hoping to create a sort of critical mass that would make everything magically fall into place and make sense. That was not the case."

She laughs. "So what provokes the awakening?"

"In me it was knowing that something was wrong. I felt that everything was wrong and I really wanted to know what the truth was. That's what awakening is. It's just truth awareness. Questioning everything around you until you get to the truth."

"What do you mean by truth, exactly. Doesn't everyone have their own version of the truth?"

"No," I say, shaking my head. "Because there is only one truth and that is simply that you are conscious. Everything else is a belief".

"And how do you get to that truth? You could argue that every teenager questions what they don't agree with. For example, their parents' curfew."

"They do do it but then they stop."

"So that's the thing, they stop?"

"When we are children I think we have a different relationship to the Truth. But then your parents put all their shit on you. Society puts all its shit on you, and it doesn't feel right. You start to construct the self in order to relate at a very young age. I think that's why kids in puberty start to rebel. They are fighting back a little. Think about how present children are. Think about how present, happy and light they are. That's because they don't have any sense of self yet. They haven't been burdened with expectation yet, they simply exist. Once burdened, no matter how hard they fight, they all surrender because it's all they know.

"But if you keep fighting, you keep questioning. And you will eventually discover something in your life that you disapprove of – the crack in reality that you can't unsee – and that will be the spark to start the fire under your ass. It is different for every single person. *Why do I have to work a nine-to-five job? Why do I have to work in finance for the rest of my life? Why do I have to take care of my sick mother? Why do I have to inherit my family's business?* Something. Anything. But most people don't stop to question. And if you don't question, you don't wake the beast."

"They just go *Why me?* and carry on with it, anyway?"

I nod. "They just carry on with the shit that's thrown at them instead of looking deeper for the true reality of the situation. *Do I HAVE to do this?* That's what I held on to and that's how I kept going. I tried to follow social norm and social structure but it just didn't work. The resistance was always there. So I surrendered and stopped fighting it. I went my own way."

"And where did it take you – that choice to go your

own way? Because the trouble with some teenagers, or children, even, is that they can go their own way but they might run straight under a truck or something."

"Then maybe that's exactly what they need to do."

She laughs. "Really?"

"Maybe that's it, maybe that will be the punch in the face that tells them what reality is. Most people don't start to question reality until something becomes unsatisfactory."

"Intolerable, rather. If it's only unsatisfactory, most will keep going."

"Right. They need something to initiate the change and for some people that may never come. For others, it can be something quite small, and for others, still, something massive. For me, it was an overall anger at the fact that everything I saw didn't make sense. That everything seemed wrong. I wanted to figure out what the hell was going on. By focusing my time and thoughts on tearing apart the beliefs that were being imposed on me, I came to realize that they weren't real. That no belief is actually true. They are called beliefs for a reason."

Sandra frowns. I can almost hear her processing. "But it's quite a big jump from that to say that all religion is not true. You could argue that the stories in the Bible are metaphors or allegories. Spiritual teaching dressed up in story."

"Yes, that's fine but it's not truth."

"Aren't stories mirrors or paths to a truth? A narrative

example of compassion or love?"

"That's emotion. That's not truth."

"Can you explain the difference?"

"Emotion is the sensation the False Self experiences in relation to a desire or previous experience. It's one of the many clutches Maya has on us. Truth is that those aren't real. They aren't you, even if you are the one experiencing them."

"But what about a truth like... you're sitting on the floor here?"

"Am I?" I laugh. "It's little steps as you go through the process. I tore apart Christianity as I knew it but the more I looked, nothing about it was true to me. And it took some time to settle into that.

"Then I went further, into Buddhism. I focused on it and, again, I could tear the incongruities apart. It wasn't true. None of it was true. It's a nice idea, world peace, happiness, compassion, non attachment, but none of it was true. *The truth is much bigger than that. Non-attachment is the result of waking up, not the way to get there.* Again, you settle into that new perspective and move on.

"It just gets bigger and bigger until nothing seems to be true. Then you start to question *OK, if none of this is real then am I real? Is this whole experience I'm having real?* When you run out of things to tear apart. The only thing left is yourself. That's the only thing left to destroy. So you apply the same process of questioning to everything you think you are. And, slowly, you start to tear away the parts of yourself that you think are true."

"So where did your process of tearing apart the self start?" she probes. "When did you turn from the outside world to yourself, and what provoked that shift? What was the first thing that fell away under your scrutiny?"

I smile, remembering. "Well, the first thing that fell away was the concept of spirituality and religion as a whole. That was the first thing that collapsed because that's what was consuming me. There has to be something, so I went on a spiritual path to find it. But I discovered that none of that is real, none of those things are true."

"Perhaps. But that's still the outside. When did it go from the outer world to touching the ego? Challenging the basic construct of self?"

"When I realized that nothing outside was real," I laugh. "Let me tell you another one of my little mystical experiences. I try to always be in a sort of deep state of thought. Not thought like *What am I going to have for dinner tonight? The weather is so nice today.* That's wasted thought. That's bullshit. I'm talking about thought-questions. Investigative thinking."

"Active thinking."

I nod. "Very active thinking. Not passively playing with my thoughts – but really running through the jungle with active thought as my only weapon. I go through periods where this kind of thinking is really intense and then I take breaks. I was in one of these intense states and was super focused on what was going on around me. At that time I was really focused on Maya because I always only understood her as a concept, the way I was taught to understand her. They teach Maya to you conceptually, but that doesn't mean you can grasp the reality of what it is."

"It is difficult to grasp a Goddess, let alone one who is weaving a kind of living dream."

"Well, she's not actually a Goddess. That's just the way we are taught to understand it – a way to represent what Maya might be.

"Anyway, I was walking along the beach focusing on the concept of Maya. I was really trying to understand why, if I know Maya isn't real, I could still see everything around me. I was trying to create the separation of Maya and Beyond Maya. All of a sudden, out of nowhere, my whole world became two dimensional. Any idea of depth in my visual spectrum disappeared. Everything sucked in and became flat, like I was looking at a screen.

"Then, something started to happen to that very flat sky. Imagine an abandoned building where the inner walls have been wallpapered. Imagine no one has been in that building for over a century so the wallpaper is rolling down off the walls. That's what started happening to the sky, to the landscape. It literally started to unroll, unravel, if you will, from itself. It was falling apart. There was even a plane flying through the air at the time and along with the sky, it collapsed, crumbled and disappeared.

"I was in emptiness.

Gianuario, my husband, was still there. We were together but he didn't exist. Nothing around me existed. It didn't disappear as much as it crumbled out of existence."

"And behind it? Behind the crumbling wall?" Sandra asks.

"Nothing!"

"Nothing?"

I nod.

"What about sound? There was no sound? No roar on the other side of silence?"

"Nope! There was nothing at all." I take a deep breath. "And that's when I truly started to see Maya and the concept became real. But it only did that because I didn't stop with my intent. Intent and focus are the only things that are going to get you there. Not sitting in meditation. Not yoga. Those things create the space for you to think and act but they don't give you the result of awakening. Only consistent, active thought and action do that."

So You, Brahman and Maya are at a yoga lesson. Halfway through the class you show Brahman and Maya that you can now put your foot behind your head, while asking them "Is this it? Is this where Atman is?" They both just smile and laugh. Maya leans in to Brahman, whispering "See? It's working!"

He was fucking sparkling

"I would say any behavior that is not the status quo is interpreted as insanity, when in fact, it might actually be enlightenment. Insanity is sorta in the eye of the beholder."
- *Chuck Palahniuk, author*

Sandra and I are talking about role playing games and seeing with your real eyes.

"Ever since my visual spectrum changed," I explain, "being in what we call the real world is like playing a video game. I loved playing video games when I was a kid. I particularly liked role playing games like *The Legend of Zelda* because when you are adventuring on the game and you are supposed to move in a certain direction or do a certain thing at a certain place, the image on the screen always looks different. The bricks on the wall you are supposed to bomb are lightly colored, so they stand out a little bit. Or, if you're supposed to go on a side quest, at the point you deviate from the path you might see a squirrel but it's illuminated differently. There are always these visual signs telling you what to do.

"The same thing happens now when I walk around town. When I see something and I know the universe wants me to move towards it, it always has a little sparkle to it. It has a bit of extra light or odd shading. It looks different. But that's only because I look with my real eyes. It's hard to explain but my whole visual field changed after the Maya experience. It's different now. Even sitting here looking at you, everything seems two dimensional.

"When I see something new coming up in my life, I also see/feel it with my intuition. It's like I see a light around things that are important to pay attention to. The hint, the cue if you like, is always there, embedded into our reality and encouraging us to move toward it. But most people don't see it because they are so distracted."

"Can you give an example?" Sandra asks.

"When I got Gumbo, my dog, I was walking down the sidewalk and 50 meters away I saw this little ball of glowing light. As we approached, out bounced this puppy. I knew immediately he was ours and was going to come home with us. The owner told us a sad story about how she rescued a female dog only to find out it was pregnant and since it's a breed that some assholes like to train to fight she didn't know what to do with all the puppies because she didn't want them to fall into the wrong hands. So now she's stuck with a sick mother and seven puppies that she can't afford to keep and was at her wit's end.

"It was only right that Gumbo came home with us, but before we even met him I had created the intent to have him in my life by actively looking for what I wanted – another dog for Frida. Frida is my rescue dog and, because she was abused, she socializes better with other dogs and humans when she has a fellow dog companion. I had put out the intent several months in advance. I went to shelters and put the word out that I was looking to adopt another dog. I told the universe what I wanted with my actions and intent.

"Then the universe conspired to make it happen. When the elements were all in place, she threw it in my face. There was no doubt about it because that puppy was fucking sparkling."

Take a deep breath

"The true value of a human being can be found in the degree to which he has attained liberation from the self."
- *Albert Einstein, physicist*

"Okay, what were we talking about?" I ask Sandra, again. I seem to forget a lot of things now and have to constantly ask where we left off last time. My memory isn't what it used to be – and it's not just age. When we are having these conversations it feels like a different part of me is speaking now.

"We were talking about how in your life you often have to do things twice for them to work out," she reminds me.

"Yes. Even when starting my own business. My first attempt was a hotel. After 10 months that failed. Thankfully!"

She laughs. "I didn't know that."

"My second attempt was a yoga school and I had the keys within one week. That's what I mean by creating the intention by action. I knew I wanted to open my own business and I knew I wanted it to be community based, but I didn't know much more than that. I thought I wanted to open a hotel, but I got it wrong. That kind of thinking doesn't always work out the first time, but it seems to work out the second."

"The first business you wanted to create was a hotel?" Sandra asks with a puzzled look on her face. "That's quite different from wanting to open a yoga school."

"Completely, but I wanted a hotel because I knew the business very well and I wanted to move forward in my life financially speaking. I was in my early 30s and I wanted to do something bigger. So I put the intent out that this was what I wanted. I was clearly going in the wrong direction but I didn't know that at the time because I wasn't aware enough of what it meant to be obstructed. But the intent was there and it was strong. *This is what I want and I'm going to go for it.*

"It failed.

"However, within two weeks of changing my direction I was on a completely different path. I had only done this on the advice of a dear friend who reminded me that had I gone into the hotel business I would probably have lost all connection to yoga because I would have been consumed by the hotel. He suggested I shift my focus to something that was more in line with who I really was, or, at least, who I thought I was.

"I made a deal with him, my friend, not my True Self, that I would shift my focus for two weeks. I would let go of the hotel, since it had fallen through anyway, and I would shift my focus to yoga.

"Within seven days I had the keys to the first studio. It happened that fast. I didn't have to do anything but shift my focus.

"That's what I was saying earlier. When I have pure intent, and it's not ego based or something not aligned to my true nature, I act on it. And by acting on it, it manifests."

Sandra smiles. "But how do you know when something is coming from a place of true intent and not coming from ego?"

"I think that comes once you know how to separate yourself from your ego. Or better yet, when you become aware of what the ego is, and by that I mean your complete false sense of self.

"How I tell the difference between the two is based on feeling. I go a lot with feeling, not emotion, but by feeling into what I see and what I experience. For instance, something that is ego driven would be based around money or material or be something that is simply not aligned with your natural life flow. Like, I need a big house with a swimming pool and two extra bathrooms and three guest bedrooms. Sure, you may need those things if you are trying to have a family of swimmers move in with you, but if that's not the case then it really doesn't play a natural role in your personal life development. It's just something you want for no other reason than wanting it."

"So desire isn't enough? Desire for anything – even awakening – is not enough?"

"No. Not at all. YOU HAVE TO ACT!" I laughingly yell. I do that a lot. Things get humorously intense in these kinds of discussions.

"What about acting on a desire – even if it's not a desire of true intent? Does that somehow push you further on your life path?"

"That rather depends on the nature of your desire. That's what I'm trying to get at. Is your desire based on the ego or is it something that you truly feel that you want in the natural direction of your life? And in saying that, I'm not saying I think you necessarily have a predestined path or direction in your life. You are here to experience. You can't control the winds but you can steer the ship."

Sandra pauses a moment to think. "What about with people? Relationships with people, for example. Sometimes you can think that a person is in your life for a reason and that's what you truly want and it's good for both of you. And it might be true. But sometimes it can be complete delusion on your part. How do you separate what's really good for you and what's just a statement of intent?"

"This just brings you back to being focused. If you are aware enough, the universe will do it for you."

"Wait. Earlier you said that you go with your feelings. You go with what you see and what you feel. . . "

"I said *feeling*, not to be confused with emotional *feelings*."

She laugh. "Yes, that's it. You made the distinction between the two. Can you talk a little about that? How do you tell them apart?"

"I've always had a strong intuition, but it's something that people can learn."

"Intuition, like a gut instinct?"

"More or less. Going with your gut instead of going with your thoughts."

"I was interested in what you just said about going with your feeling and not your emotion," Sandra says, leaning in. "I want to look at that separation of feeling and emotion. When you clarified *feeling*, you said *feeling* in terms of what I feel in my body, my intuition, what I see, but you didn't use the word *perception* which was the word Aldous Huxley used. The doors of perception being sensory awareness. So I was wondering if that was intentional?"

"No, it wasn't intentional at all. I've never read his books." I laugh. "We can talk about *perception* so long as

GET YOUR HEAD OUT OF YOUR ASANA

intuition is included, too."

"Let's go back to the idea of emotions and feeling. What is the difference? Or maybe we should start by talking about what an emotion is."

"Emotions to me are fear based. Always."

She widens her eyes. "Even love?"

"Especially love. It's a reflection of the fear of being alone. You think *I'm in love, so I'm no longer alone. That's awesome. I'm in love.*

"We all act out of fear," I continue. "Everything we do is out of fear. Fear of what? Fear of not knowing what the hell is going on, fear of dying, fear of no self, etc. The basic big questions. Religion, what does it do? It satiates fear. It tells you what's going to happen when you die. It tells you how to live your life.

"But the difference between emotions and feelings... My feelings come from someplace deep inside of me, whereas my emotions do not. My emotions feel like they are from the False Self. They are very reactionary. The True Self doesn't have emotions. It only has the experience itself, awareness, consciousness."

Sandra sits back in her chair and thinks. "In traditional Chinese medicine theory it's interesting because all emotions, good or bad, are seen as being deregulated q i *(pronounced chee)*. Qi has been defined as energy, but is perhaps more correctly translated as "smooth or correct functioning." So, assuming the qi in someone's body was actually flowing in a correct and natural way, any kind of emotion, good or bad, would be seen to deregulate that. And if that emotion were to continue and the body wasn't able to rebalance itself, it would become pathological.

"The idea that the body has a sense of order, consciousness or awareness that can be perturbed by emotion - but is in no way the same thing as *an emotion*, is interesting, don't you think?"

I nod.

She continues. "What I think we see a lot of today is a split between the heart and the head. Some people are completely in one and oblivious to the other. They use will to override what their true voice, or feeling, is trying to tell them.

"I suppose if you have already awakened then it's easy to tell the difference between feeling and emotion. But if you are in a place of trauma, for instance, and that trauma happened very early on in your childhood, how do you find the difference between emotion that comes from that deep place of trauma, and feelings that come from your True Self? I mean, some people dissociate from the trauma so they aren't even aware of the trauma influencing and triggering their entire perception of the world."

That's a big question. I smile to myself, wondering where to start. "Are you asking me how to get past that or how to see the difference between the two?"

"How to tell the difference between emotion and

feeling, or emotion and perception. How do you tell the difference? How do you know when a feeling is real and should be given attention and when it' s just an emotion coming from the False Self?" She frowns. "I guess that's what I'm really asking."

"You know because of how it affects your state of mind. When I feel something that I can really say comes from my true nature there are no questions. I don't think about it. I feel it. It comes with a sense of peace and understanding.

"However, if I experience an emotion, it's bombarded with thoughts at the same time. If it's an emotion, let's use love as an example, you love someone but you don't feel content in that love. Your brain is still going crazy. Do they feel like I feel? Do they love me back? What do I do next? Where am I going? What is this? Blah blah blah... It's a mess!

"If a feeling comes from your True Self it comes with no baggage at all. It's pure, clean and delivered. That's the feeling I'm talking about.

"If you are connected to a feeling emotionally, from your False Self, you can't rationalize it. You are lost, going in circles in your head about how to process what you are feeling. And that's because it is emotion based. Is that clear?"

I begin to feel that this part of the conversation might not come out right. The process is still very fresh in my mind and, as we are having these discussions, I feel I'm speaking from a part of me that's about to be torn away, too.

Sandra looks at me as if she can feel my doubts. "So, in

the context of a relationship," she clarifies, "if there is real love between you, there is a sense of calm and connectedness that's not worried in any way by intellectualization or questions or a barrage of other thoughts?"

"Yes. And that calm clarity comes to your whole life once you get here, where I am."

"I'd like that!" She laughs. "But what about something like when your job's not working out and you start asking yourself a lot of questions about what to do next or where to go? There needs to be some sort of thinking in terms of *What am I doing with my career?* Or even *What am I doing with my life?*"

"Does there? If you don't know what to do next then don't do anything. What I try to teach people is to simply pay attention. The universe is constantly offering you hints, ideas, clues...like the video game vision I spoke of before. That's how I see things and everyone can see things like this – if they just paid attention. You are constantly being given signs and signals so if you don't know what to do, you aren't paying attention, and that's okay because most of the time none of us are.

"It helps if you pull back and breathe. Breath is so important. Every time I meet with a new client, I teach them how to breath because that's where it starts anyway. Nothing will change if you aren't breathing properly. Breath is truly fundamental in making any sort of transition from where you are at in your life – whether it be physical or mental.

"When you are breathing properly you leave the fight or flight mode. Your physiology changes, the vibration in your brain calms down and then you can pay attention. You can look. You can start to change the things you see.

"All of us are stressed. Constantly stressed. Either it's mental stress from social pressure or physical stress from too much activity or whatever bullshit is happening around us at the time. But if you breathe properly, you begin to feel properly as well. It's truly the first thing I do when I meet with new clients. First I let them come into the room and just fucking *blehhhhhhhhhhhhhhhhhhhhhhhhhhhhhh!!!!!!!!!!!!!!* I let *them* unload all their shit on me. *Why are you here? That's* the point of that question. *Tell me now, get it all out. Blehhhhhhhhhhhhhhhhhhhhhh!!!!! And then what do you want? Blehhhhhhhhhhhhhhhhhhh!!!!! Yes, just get it out!* I let them regurgitate all of this and when they are done I correct their posture, I correct their breath. We talk about what they have said before and then we look back at it."

Sandra takes a big breath. Very consciously. She looks at me and grins. "So, once you've corrected the breath and the posture," she says, "and you go back into what they have said, do your new clients often see the contradictions or inconsistencies for themselves? Do they see themselves and their stories differently just with the correction of posture and breath?"

"Their vibration and awareness change, so it's a start. They can then see things from a less emotional perspective."

"And from this space of calm, you start to talk?"

"Yes. That's the first thing I get them to do because for most people our sessions initially revolve around work. Work is what we do the most. It's actually where we spend the majority of our time awake. And a lot of people who come to me come because something isn't going well for them at that time.

"But that's not it, really, because work is just a big part of your life. When your career isn't working out or going well, it means your life, in general, isn't going well. So I often use work as the point of focus to start things moving. I tell clients that when they are at work and they start feeling unhappy with a situation to just stop whatever it is they are doing and come back to their breath. Come back to their posture, come back to their body. And once they are fully present in that moment, to ask themselves how that changes the way they see their situation. It starts there. Breath is the most important thing. If you aren't breathing properly, you aren't going to think properly. You are only going to think in a state of stress. And nobody makes good decisions or feels anything genuine in a state of stress."

•

Time Out

I'd like to stress, to you, the reader, the importance of meditation as a breathing exercise. The first thing you should do every morning as soon as you roll out of bed is to sit quietly and connect to your breath. That's all meditation really is.

We are simply just finding a nice place to focus, and the side effect of that focus is a quiet mind. That quiet mind is where the process of waking up begins.

Take a moment now to really breathe. Put the book down, sit up straight, close your eyes and see how deep, long and slow you can make your breath become. Think about breathing into your belly, not your chest. Put one of your hands on your belly if it helps to have an extra point of focus. Take 10 very long deep breaths and then come back to us.

Anytime you need a break to process, just put the book down, close your eyes and take a few deep breaths.

•

There is a huge difference

"To become different from what we are,
we must have some awareness of what we are."
- *Eric Hoffer, philosopher*

Sandra and I are discussing coaching clients and conscious breathing.

"I can understand how important that breathing exercise might be in a one-on-one coaching session," She says. "And even at work when something shakes you, you can go back into your breath to ground yourself. In both examples, it's you and the situation. But what happens when you are in a group? You're going along, having a good time, and then suddenly you start doing things that aren't really what you intended to do. Or you know that you are going off track because you got carried with the flow of the group. Do you, while still in the group, start trying to breathe and reconnect to yourself or do you just walk away?"

I respond immediately. "I would leave the group! I would just leave."

"Well," she laughs, "you are a solitary creature."

"Maybe. But I would still just walk away. Like you should do with most things in your life that don't feel right. You are either in your flow or you aren't."

"So that's it? When you are in your flow, there is a sense of calm and your breath and posture are correct? And when you're not in your flow, there are too many thoughts or a feeling of discomfort or unease?"

"Not always. But it's good to start paying attention to these things. Something could just be where it's not supposed to be. People could actually be 'sort of' in their flow and not be aware of it. Or they could be completely out of their flow and not be aware of that, either. And both can happen because, for whatever reason, people are not actually present."

She thinks about that. "So, you think you can still be in your flow and not be aware of it? Just like you can be obstructed and not be aware of that, either? It's not that if you aren't aware, you aren't in your flow?"

"By becoming aware you just make sure that your flow is consistent. You become more aware of what's going on around you, and then you can learn to encourage and influence what is going on. That brings us back to co-creation, but more about that later."

"I was thinking of children and how it's true that they are totally in their flow until they have had too much sugar, or get tired, or something obstructs them and then they collapse."

"It's the same thing with adults. We collapse because we are no longer in our flow. That collapse can manifest as pain, sickness, hyperactivity, anxiety, unease. Think burn out. But, essentially, we are just not in our flow.

"That flow is often compromised, wrecked even, during adolescence when, depending on how you handle things, you actually stop growing consciously. If you stop growing, you get stuck. That's when it all begins. You see it with children a lot. They are fine until something starts to influence their reality like a dramatic change in the family situation. Kids are very quick to come back though. Adults are not."

"Do you think that's partly to do with our intellectualization of things?" She asks. "Things go wrong and then we start inventing excuses for why that happened, or blaming someone for it, or putting something somewhere it doesn't belong. Why do we get stuck?"

"For one, we don't know any better, we think *Okay, this is just how it is.* We are told as children that things are different when you're an adult. That life is about responsibility, *blah blah blah.* All bullshit! All lies. Yet you think *I'm a grown up now and this is just how life is.* Shit doesn't work, you don't get what you want, and things get in the way. But that's not true. Things work exactly how they are supposed to work, nothing gets in the way of that – except yourself. We are taught as adults that life is hard but actually life is very fucking easy." I take a deep breath. "All you have to do is survive and then die. Who cares? It's over. It's really that easy. But getting to the place where you find that ease is a whole other story. That's why this is such a hard topic to talk about. It's so vast and there is no checklist of things to do to get here. You have to arrive to find out.

"Maybe as I get further along in my own process and have more interactions with people who are trying to change their lives I will start to see more patterns. But up to now, every individual I have talked to about awakening and flow has been completely different. And the catalyst that's pushing them forward is also completely different – the thing that brings about their need for change, that opened their eyes to the fact that the world we are living in isn't real. I can say that there is this particular moment in every story, a moment that pushes you, unequivocally, towards the truth – but what that moment is and how to get there, I don't know."

The conversation drops for a minute. We sip at our tea, letting the words and thoughts around us settle. I realize the dust is also still settling on my own process. I begin to see more clearly when my personal awakening from the False Reality began. Now I see the action that started the process of self destruction for me. It was a burnout of sorts. I was overworked, but since I love what I do, I didn't know it. I couldn't tell. The snap came though, almost completely unannounced, and that began the process of me destroying my False Self.

Prior to that, I was awake but not enlightened. There is a huge difference. One can be awake within the False Reality or one can go further and awaken from it altogether.

What got me to where I am now was complete surrender. I completely relinquished myself of this life. I dropped everything and just left, both physically and mentally. I went to a lovely little ashram in France where you can disappear – live in silence, do yoga, read books, be alone. And though I wasn't gone for long physically, I was alone and isolated long enough to let the universe take over. As it did, I realized how sweet true surrender can be. Some of us try for this on vacation, but that's nothing compared to just letting go of life – completely. Dropping the reins and stopping. For good. The False Self had created all this busy-ness my entire life, and I wasn't having it anymore. It no longer served me

YOUR HEAD OUT OF YOUR ASANA

and I didn't want it. Upon my return, the way back into what was my normal life was a slow, arduous process. Only then did the False Self begin to actually die.

...

Sandra's been watching me come back to myself. "I want to go back to this idea of the intellect versus the emotions," she says. "I think it's very present as a dichotomy in the West versus the East. For example, in the East they say that they are more about being, and the West is more about doing and thinking. I don't know how accurate that is, but I'm curious as to what you think. In the Chinese tradition they have something called Self Cultivation. That's the cultivation of the body and the mind. You cultivate both at the same time through things like qigong, which is a combination of physical exercises and breath control. Also through study, correct action and correct connection. We've talked about feeling and perception and the sense of a higher reality, but I'm wondering where the mind comes into play in your experience of awakening – and if it's even important?"

"The mind is super important in the process of awakening because the only thing that actually pushes you further along the path is active thought."

"So what, for you, is active thought and what is non active thought?"

"Non active thought is "*It's such a nice day today, and so was yesterday and then I was in the park, and I was eating a nice fresh pineapple that I bought at the local supermarket. I don't like that market but it's the closest one to my house. Am I lazy for not going to the better fruit and vegetable markets?*" This sort of a non-stop mental conversation with yourself that goes nowhere is non-active thought. It's wasted bullshit thinking. Active thought is looking at something for what it truly is and discerning that for yourself."

"So, the pineapple in the supermarket?"

"It's just a pineapple. That's it. And it stops there. It's funny, when I'm thinking, I'm actively thinking about something. I'm thinking about the concept of Maya, my existence, my place in the world, something true, something real. If I'm not thinking about those things there is silence. I no longer think about nonsense."

"Silence, that's interesting. So active thinking is actually more restful."

"Completely. Thought is only a tool to achieve something."

"And we've gotten into a place where we run on constant thought – thought, counter thought, argument, justification, guilt and blame."

"Yes, our thinking is always on. It runs and runs, just going in circles about bullshit and never getting to a point. Never reaching a resolution. Just piling more shit on top of you."

"Do you think that's because we don't have a practice to still the mind? We don't have an integrated natural practice of meditation or letting go?"

"Not really. This kind of thinking could happen in meditation as well. You could sit there for half an hour and only think about your day!"

"But one would say that that's not real meditation."

"No, not at all."

"But I know people who do it that way and call it meditation." Sandra says. "It's exhausting, this state where our minds are on all the time? How did we get here?"

"Fear. When you become silent you are forced to consider the big questions like *Who am I? What am I? When am I going to die? What the fuck is going on?* We avoid those things by getting lost and consumed by our lives and emotions. Distractions. It's all distraction."

"Back to Maya on the beach and the wall paper, unraveling." She sighs.

"YES! That's exactly it. It's all distraction. Let's see who can distract themselves the best. That's the world we live in. That's it. I see fear in everyone's eyes. Everyone. It's part of the zombie state that you see in the shell of people when they don't know their True Self. Everything in their lives is orchestrated by fear. Even if the people living that way deny it or don't recognize it themselves."

"Some admit it, but don't do anything about it."

"Yes, some people will admit it and then say that's the way it is. But that alone doesn't mean they want to change. It's as if they don't actually understand what they are saying."

"So, say you're reading this and suddenly you realize that *Yes, I am afraid of everything!* Then what?" Sandra asks. "What do you do once you recognize it or accept it? What's the way out of the fear? Some people talk about the polarity of being in terms of Fear versus Love. You are either reacting to the world from a place of Fear or from a place of Love. What would you say about leaving fear? How do you do that?"

"The way I have always done it – by running towards it!!"

We laugh.

"No, seriously," I continue. "If something scares me I run to it. Actually, I run at it."

"Because you think it's there and you might as well deal with it straight on?"

"Yes, and then I can move on. But running towards fear is also an exercise in destroying the False Self because it is the False Self who is afraid."

"But most people, even the bravest, are not going to run headlong at whatever they fear the most. But they might gently edge their way towards it. What would you say to them?"

"Nothing is going to change until you confront fear."

"Is it just a matter of time? A matter of how much time you allow the fear to control you and how much time you take to confront it?"

"Timing? No."

"For example, if I'm afraid of death. I can sit here and be afraid of death or I can walk straight into death."

"Well, that's the basic human experience. We're all afraid of death so we are just distracting ourselves from the fact that we are going to die until we die. Then, when we die, it's like, *Oh fuck, what did I do that for when I could have been living my life?*

"By waking up you can have that experience much earlier. You can evolve as a person and actually enjoy the world around you instead of being afraid of it. I get surprises every day and it just makes life magical. Wonderful."

Sandra's not following me. She's stuck on something she didn't get an answer to earlier. I can feel the restlessness of her thoughts. I stop speaking and wait.

"How would I confront death? I mean, if death is the ultimate thing that everyone is afraid of. What would I do with it?"

"You just have to accept the fact that–"

She cuts me off. "So it's not about throwing yourself off a bridge or bungee jumping or scaring yourself to death?"

"Maybe..."

"I'm just wondering if that's it for some people. Deliberate risk-taking is their way of confronting death."

"Well, I've had two near death experiences. One that I remember and one that I don't completely remember because I was so young. Near death experiences help with this kind of process. But they are temporary. Like a window opening for a short time. When you speak to people who have had near death experiences, they wake up for about a week or two. Maybe a month, if they are lucky. I think we've talked about this before. They wake up briefly and they are truly awake. They are more alert, aware of life, aware of their life... and then *wroooooop!* They just fall back to where they were."

"Because they are afraid of what they see?"

"Yes. That's why you have to stay focused. For a long time. To this day, I remind myself daily of my mortality."

"How do you do that?"

"Every time I leave the house I leave as if I'm leaving for the last time. I actually wave goodbye to my house and I leave as if when I get to the end of the street I am going to get hit by a bus. That's how I live every day of my life and it keeps me very happy with what I have. This experience is all we have. That's it. When you not only realize how brief life is, but can actually understand it conceptually, you begin to realize how foolish you have been to sweat all the small stuff.

"I tell people this all the time and they are like, *Yeah, you're right.* And the moment they leave the conversation they go right back to where they were. Lost. Afraid. Over thinking.

"I keep death in my face. You should be looking at it constantly – your whole fucking quest. You should know that at the end of this road is Death. It's all over. If more people embraced the fact that the only thing they have to look forward to in their physical life is dying, they would enjoy every moment of life they have along the way – bitter or sweet – and realize that they are not this body or mind. It's very simple. I'm aware of my mortality at almost every moment. That's the only reality of this physical life. Nobody knows what's going on around us. I've experienced that everything we take to be real is not. I've seen it with my own eyes. But I'm still here. Just because I know it's not real doesn't mean that I can leave either.

"All I know is that I am here, and here isn't real. I have also learned that I can influence what seems real, so that's what I'm going to do. And while I'm doing it, I'll keep in mind that everything is temporary – which makes it even more confusing."

We laugh.

"But when you accept that," I continue, "When you accept that you honestly don't know anything – and just let go and surrender to it, you find yourself in some sort of weird energy field. A flow of things moving around you, that you realize you have a little influence over. The more you are aware of what's going on around you, the easier it becomes.

"By embracing your death you can no longer be attached to physical things because you already know that life isn't permanent. That's one of the things I like about Buddhism, the mandalas. They spend hours, days, weeks, making these big beautiful designs just to wash them away. That's how you should be every single morning. Every single day when you look in the mirror, embrace the fact that you are dying.

"We age. People don't seem to like aging but I love it. I love the feeling of my body getting older and changing because it's the only experience we have, really, being in a body, this body, and watching it rise and fall. That's it. There is nothing more. And when you know that, you don't get so involved in your personal dramas or life problems. You stay centered, present in yourself.

"Having lived like this for some time, I am beginning to see patterns and the structure of things going on around me. This perspective gives me an awareness of when things are out of flow or going to go bad. So long as I'm paying attention I will see them coming.

"Anyone can do this. When the separation of self is achieved, the only thing left is consciousness. Emotions and stress leave with the False Self. You become the true observer. Consciousness itself."

It only takes one spark

"Enlightenment is man's release from his self-incurred
tutelage. Tutelage is man's inability to make use
of his understanding without direction from another.
Self-incurred is this tutelage when its cause lies not
in lack of reason but in lack of resolution and courage
to use it without direction from another. Sappers aude!
'Have courage to use your own reason!'
That is the motto of enlightenment."
- *Immanuel Kant, philosopher*

We are sitting again on the floor at the small round
glass table in the studio lounge for our weekly lunch
discussion about the process of waking up and
enlightenment.

Sandra launches in. "The first step is the fire."

"Hmmm?" I have a mouth full of food and I've totally forgotten where we left off.

Sandra hasn't and she pulls me right back to the exact point we were working towards. "The first step is the fire. If you're not burning inside you don't have a motivation to change."

I must look blank.

"That's where we agreed we'd start from," she reminds me. "The last time we met."

Sandra sees this book project from a completely different perspective than I do – and that's exactly what I need. At the beginning of this project, I told the universe that if it wanted this book to happen then it had to make it happen. I have a hard time going back to places in my consciousness that I have been to before, and as I shine the light on where my clients are in their own personal process, so Sandra shines the light for me – to make sure we are guiding this dialogue in the right direction for the reader. Thank you universe, and thank you, Sandra!

"Oh yes, *that* fire..." I smile. "What I mean is that you can have a sense of curiosity, but that you know what is behind it. You know why you want to know more. You may want to get into yoga, eastern philosophy, shamanism, psychedelics or something like that. But behind that interest is something bigger – and that's what you need to find."

"What lies beyond your curiosity."

"Yes. What is the motivation behind the curiosity? What are you really asking for? What do you want to know? Curiosity is questioning things. But when I think of curiosity, I think of it more in a playful way, a frolicking way. Curiosity isn't what you use when you are tearing your world, your false identity and your ego apart."

"So curiosity is like exploring. It's like, *Let's see what happens if I press that. What's under there?*"

"Yes."

"But the fire you are talking about is something else – the motivation to change."

"Think of it as curiosity with force!" I say. "The force is very important because you can be curious about anything. Let's use shamanism, as an example. It's one thing to be curious about it and read about it and study it and maybe attend a workshop or two. That is curiosity.

"But what is it you really want from all that? What's your motivation? What's your goal? What's the endgame you are looking for that makes you curious about it in the first place? Is it that you want to talk to the spirits of land, sky and sea? Or are you searching for inner peace? Or is it that you like to trip out on herbal drugs? Are you trying to escape your False Reality or plunge headfirst further into it? The more questions you ask, the closer you get to your true motivation. And that motivation, that fire, becomes pure intent.

"As I mentioned before, the fire in me was that I simply couldn't believe anything anyone told me. Nothing seemed to make sense – and I wanted it to. As much as I researched I found nothing that rang true – and that was my fire. I wanted to know the truth. Your need to know drives your curiosity – whatever path it takes you on."

"So your need for the truth was the stimulus, because the real fire must have been the thought of living in a world where nothing made sense. Where you didn't have a grip on anything. That was the fire."

"Good point!" I nod.

She continues, "Because the fire usually comes from a clear space and it's usually based on survival. *I can't go on like this. Something has to change!*"

"That's it. You hit the nail on the head. That's a perfect definition of the fire. *I cannot carry on like this, this is not my reality. What is this I'm experiencing? This cannot continue.* So, yes, exactly!"

"I think we mentioned before that illness can be a good catalyst for change. You cannot continue the way you are going so you have to change. And if those changes can be maintained, your life continues in a different direction – even if it is only living with the knowledge that life itself is temporary and, therefore, precious."

"Yes. Unfortunately the changes incurred with illness are often not long-lasting."

"How do you then go about maintaining a desire and an intention to change?" She asks. "How do you stoke the fire? How do you keep it burning? You can have a shock that makes you go, *I can't do this anymore, I want to change.* You do it for a month or two months and then it starts unraveling."

"It's hard for me to answer from personal experience because I never had to stoke my fire because it was already so intense. My own disbelief in the world around me was a constant reminder of what I couldn't find and I guess that kept the fire alive."

Sandra laughs. "But what about the students or clients that you have? Many of them must come with a desire to change, but maybe without a fire strong enough to keep that desire on track, or push it past curiosity."

"You have to get to the point where your current state is no longer acceptable. It's not even tolerable. It's just not possible to be like this, to think like this, to live like this. You have to get to that state. I truly can't express this point enough!"

"But does that always have to be through something negative? *I can't live like this anymore because my body won't move or I'm miserable.* Could it not just be a simple desire for change? A better way."

"That's what I was mentioning before. You say you want to change but why? If you don't know, you just want change, then you need to question that desire and ask yourself why it is you want change. Or what it is you want to change. Most of us don't embrace change willingly. We want it because of something else that is happening. You know what I mean? So the desire for change alone isn't enough – you have to know what it is you actually want to change. Otherwise you're just running."

Sandra thinks that over. "Let's talk about desire, then. When you talk about desire for change what does that mean to you? How do you differentiate between desire for change and the motivation to do it? On some level they are almost the same. Where does desire become strong enough to work its way into change?"

"For me it really came when I found this world unacceptable. It was a visceral reaction. Hot, strong, fierce. That's why I called it fire. Every time I looked at the world, I couldn't see how any of it made sense, and I wouldn't stop looking until I knew more, and more and more. That's the sort of fire you need to create real change. Only changing certain aspects of your life can be extremely superficial. Changing your job, changing your house - that could also just be escapism. It's all about the motivation."

"Do you think making those superficial changes are like mirrors of a deeper spiritual desire or a sense of wanting to change? Like if you go from a world of advertising into something that's more meaningful –."

"Yoga!" I interrupt. I say this with a slight edge of sarcasm in my voice because I see it every day! "People think yoga will change their life. The truth is, it can – but only if they approach it correctly, which a lot of people don't. People do end up calmer, fitter and more flexible, but their self awareness hasn't changed in the slightest and that's the problem."

I started doing yoga because I wanted Samadhi, enlightenment. Yoga didn't get me there in the sense that I thought it would, but it did help. Owning studios and teaching for 20 years means I've met *a lot* of yoga teachers – and in my opinion, most of them shouldn't actually be teachers of yoga, at least, not in the sense of awakening their students. They are very good asana teachers but they are stuck there. The problem is, they aren't awake enough to realize it. And so they live in a beautiful, warm, soft, comfy yoga bubble believing they are waking up when they are simply asleep in a very comfortable space within Maya. And there is nothing wrong with that – but call it what it is. You will never be awakened by a teacher like that, at least not more than you would with any other form of fitness class. You might get a little more inner peace, sure – and that is a part of it. But it's part of the illusion. I'm in the business of breaking people out of the illusion, not redirecting the traffic.

Sandra coughs, politely bringing me back to our conversation. She was asking about the desire to change the ethics behind your work as part of the fire of intent. "If I am still dreaming," she asks, "and work in advertising or sales and I decide to leave that and move towards working with yoga or a holistically based medicine, is that a step in the right direction? Or is it completely irrelevant because I'm not awake yet?"

"It's irrelevant unless you know what your true motivation is. If you do it because you are unhappy with your job, fine. But why were you unhappy with your job? Why are you unhappy with things the way they are? Your choices led you to that previous point. It was clearly what you wanted because you created it. You made it happen. And you thought it would make you happy. So why didn't it? Changing your job is fine, of course. But it won't change your situation because clearly you are not happy with things the way they are – and that usually relates to more than just your job."

"And what about this notion of creation? We've talked about it before. If you're creating your dream job and it no longer makes you happy, and you choose to create another in a completely different field that you think will make you happier, is that conscious creation?"

"Those unhappy people didn't create those jobs consciously. If they were involved at all it was unconscious creation – basically the result of their previous thoughts and actions. Karma, if you will. Conscious creation is a bit further down the line. It comes very late in the process and you have to be awake first."

Sandra looks around the room, taking that in. "There are various schools of thought that talk about the world you have around you being a mirror – so if your plant is dying there is an element of you dying as well. Everything on the outside mirrors what's going on inside. Do you subscribe to that as a belief?"

"No." I point to a dead plant in the lounge. "That plant is dead but I'm still alive. To me that sort of thinking is still part of the illusion. That plant is dead. It froze. Big deal. All of those things are not true. That sort of thinking stays within the unawakened state. The False Reality."

"So, for you, in that world of non-reality or of not being awake, nothing really matters. You put in your house whatever you like because you like it. Nothing reflects or means more than that."

"Precisely."

Sandra frowns. She is trying to find a way to hold onto things, to create meaning within Maya and that's a survival mechanism of the ego.

I go on. "I do believe in things like *The Art of Tidying Up*. How you live overall is a reflection of your mental state and that's something we approach in yoga all the time. The body and the mind are reflections of each other, sure."

She lets out a long breath, clearly relieved. "Can you talk a bit about that? How do you work with that idea in yoga? The body and mind being reflections of each other."

"It usually comes down to awareness. My goal as a yoga teacher is to make people become aware of their bodies as an entry point to becoming aware of everything else around them. If you don't know your own body – the only physical thing that we have to relate to in this life and that we can somehow call our own – if you don't know how that works and how it moves, how can you have any sort of awareness about anything else? It's just not possible. For me, as a yoga teacher, that's the starting point. And that awareness begins with the breath."

I think back to the client I saw before lunch, a woman with a very round back and very high shoulders because ever since she was a child she's been hyperactive and keeps a lot of tension in the front of her body. If you try sitting like that you feel your diaphragm can't move. Her diaphragm needed releasing so she could actually breathe. I like to use neuromuscular activation techniques on my students when they feel physically stuck. It brings the focus back to the body and, before that, to the breath. If you are not able to breathe, you aren't able to live. The client came to talk about what she could do to change her life and I set her to learning to breathe again – and to watch the effects that had on her physiologically and in terms of the vibration and clarity of her thoughts. Breath was her starting point, but it is basically everyone's starting point.

"The awareness of breath and the body," Sandra muses.

"And where it gets stuck!"

"Sometimes in acupuncture we work on scars. We talk about scars as being a place where the qi doesn't run particularly well. Women who have had c-section, for example, or who have large scars as a result of other operations are often not aware of that part of their body. They can do a body scan and when they get to the area of the scar, above and below, there is nothing. When they touch that part of their body, they either can't touch the scar or the area above or below it feels numb."

I nod. "They have no more connection to that muscle anymore. I have worked with many women in my classes who have had c-sections and they cannot consciously connect to that muscle because their abdomen was completely ripped into two pieces. There is a lot of scar tissue there and the nerves no longer fire the same way. And what you took for granted as a natural physical connection to that part of your body has gone."

"Exactly! So I was wondering what happens if you know how your body works, but that there are parts of it that you have lost awareness of because of trauma of some kind?"

"What I'm trying to do is give people body and breath awareness to pull their focus back in and take them out of the brain. By taking them out of the endless chatter in their heads and focusing on their bodies, they can still their thoughts long enough to connect to their True Selves. Without that stillness, it will never happen. Things like scars or missing limbs don't really matter in this context."

"But what about the idea of trauma initiating a fire of change?" She thinks for a moment and laughs. "Is there even a way that doesn't involve trauma? I mean, a way of discipline or intention alone that allows you to get to that place?"

"Intention alone is enough. I had a cool life. I didn't

have any huge traumas other than - hmm, okay, I did have a couple of near death experiences."

"That's pretty big trauma!"

"Hahaha, not for me. Not in that sense. I had one when I was a child that I don't really remember. But it wasn't trauma that led me here. It was my need to know the truth and my own questioning."

Last night, my husband Gianuario and I were discussing how we interact with others. We are both very direct and neither of us have a tolerance for bullshit and that can make things difficult. He asked me if I had ever thought that I was autistic. He said maybe we are both autistic and that we don't really know how to communicate with other people. That really made me think for a moment. Not that I think that it's true. I have certainly never been diagnosed, but I wouldn't care if I were and it was true because I like the state of mind that I am in. I like my awareness and how I got here.

"But to go back to your question," I say. "It was never trauma that led me here. I was raised very confused, religiously speaking, but that's not a trauma. I could have just rejected spirituality all round, but I didn't because I'm inquisitive and that's what you need to be to get anywhere."

"So what's the difference between being inquisitive, having a motivation to change, and having a desire to change or a longing to change. Where do you think the lines are?"

I have to think for a moment. "When I was inquisitive

I never really wanted change in my life because my physical life had nothing to do with where my consciousness was going. Not then."

"Do you think it's like that for most people?"

"It can be but most people aren't aware of it because they are consumed with their physical lives. That's what they want to change. Changing your physical life won't change very much if you don't change your awareness and your approach to it first. Changing your awareness begins by asking *What is real?* And that's a question you need to ask until you tear everything else that is not real apart."

"So it's very much about staying in the present and questioning what you see in front of you. *Why? Why? Why?* As opposed to *Why did this happen in the past?*"

"I never reflect on the past or the future because that is a waste of time. Past and Future don't exist. Time is a man made creation. There is no proof that things move in a linear direction. The only thing we know for sure has conscious beings is that we are conscious. Nothing else can be proven to be true. Nothing at all."

Absolutely nothing

"Yoga does not transform the way we see things,
it transforms the person who sees."
- *B.K.S. Iyengar, yogi*

"Let's go back to talking about flow," Sandra says. "You talked of seeing your dog on the street, and how the dog lit up, and how you saw that as a sign that he should be with you – a sign of you essentially being in the flow, of being in the right place at the right time."

I nod.

"I'm wondering how you find the flow, and once you are there, how you stay in the flow. I'm also wondering if, by staying in the flow, you have an ability to change what is going on around you?"

"When you are in the flow of things, you feel it. You see it. Everything works. When you're not in the flow, everything seems to get in the way. Everything annoys you, hinders you or seems to slow you down. That struggle is a clear sign that you're not in the right place. Life is meant to be experienced and the act of living should be effortless."

"So, if we work with the metaphor of the fire as we mentioned before, the first step is to feed the fire?"

I laugh. "I'm not sure you can throw fuel on the way things flow."

"And that's what I was going to ask. If you are in the flow, is your fire automatically being fed? Like you have a direct connection to the life source or something?"

She is losing me a bit because being in the flow and finding the fire to break out of a False Reality are two different things. "I guess *you* could say it like that, sure."

"The idea of obstruction and flow is an important element in the creation of disease in traditional Chinese medicine."

"It's more like stop and go." I interject. "That's what I mean."

"Okay, so where do you go with things like the Law of

Attraction? 'Like attracts like' is a popular idea at the moment. If you're flowing and having the right vibration you can attract the kind of things you want into your life. Dream state or otherwise."

"That's possible," I say "but I don't like the way books like *The Secret* portray the concept of the Law of Attraction because, in the mainstream world of things, people are given the impression that if they just sit at home and think about what they want, they will attract it to them. The Law of Attraction is a real thing but not in the sense that you can get everything your ego desires just by thinking about it. At least that's not the way I experienced it. Visualizing what you want is nothing like actually waking up."

"Didn't the idea of the Law of Attraction become very popular with The Celestine Prophecy? It's always been around, but I think it became very mainstream then. That was about 20 years ago and was along the lines of synchronicity. Basically stating that if you were in the flow you could attract what you wanted. *The Secret* took it away from that, moving manifestation away from flow and closer to will. 'If I want it, I can have it.'"

I frown. "Yes, but that's just not it. You need to show the universe that you're willing to act. You can't just sit around and think I want a new (insert materialistic/emotional desire here) and then expect it to happen. It won't. You're doing nothing except thinking and that thinking is most likely to be non active thought. If you want something to change, you need to have clear intent, clear focus on what it is you want changed and then you need to take action to make the process begin. Otherwise, the universe won't take you seriously. Not at all. You need to act. You need to get off your ass and do something physical and actually start the process. Even if you fail! I tend to have to do things at least twice to get something right. It's the same thing with the Law of Attraction. It's a process. It's more about being aware of your True Self, and being aware of the nature of reality, than it is about articulating your ego's desires. If it's all just ego-based materialistic nonsense, well, good luck!"

*Maya shows Brahman her latest masterpiece.
"Look!" She proclaims. "I have created this diagram
of a tree with the branches of yoga and how to
find you. I'm going to share this with all
conscious beings who seek enlightenment."
Brahman asks, "But your job is
to do the exact opposite."
"Precisely!"*

"Part of the reason you wanted to work on this book," Sandra says, "was because in your process of waking up, nothing you read prepared you for what you found when you started to open your eyes."

I nod.

"So going back to that idea, if you were to give someone a 'Waking Up Survival Kit', you know – *This is what you need when the awakening process begins* – what would be in that kit?"

"Absolutely nothing!"

We both start laughing.

"Because," I continue, "that's one more piece of baggage to add to the pile of things that a person thinks they need from the outside world to wake up. You don't actually need anything from the outside world at all."

"You must need something."

I think about that. "First, you need to throw away everything you think you know. So I guess I would give them an empty box and a handwritten note: *Here is your empty box to begin the awakening process, becoming truth realized or whatever it is you wish to call it. Everything that you have been told is not true. Not that it's a lie, exactly, but because within the dream state, the world that we think is real, it is just another piece of Maya. Waking up is waking up from the dream of Maya.*"

Sandra laughs. "Perfect!"

"That would be my Wake Up Kit," I continue. "I don't

want to add more to the pile of what people think they need. I want to pull them out from underneath it. *Please come away from all of that and enter nothingness because that's the only truth there is.* That's it. So I have nothing to give them except to ask them to remove all the things they think they know and start over."

"If you don't want to add to the pile, then why are you writing this book?" Sandra asks.

"Ha! I'm glad you asked. Imagine your life is a boat. You're sitting peacefully inside it floating out at sea. Every new belief you acquire is a lead weight that is placed into your boat. Slowly, as you go deeper into Maya, or whatever belief system you are digging around in, your boat gets filled up with these weights until it's just about to go under. The pile has gotten so big it is taking you down with it. I see this book as a life preserver that I'm trying to throw to you to save you. To help pull you up when all of that shit starts to drag you down. So, yes, it's a part of the pile but hopefully the last piece. More in the sense that it's the straw that breaks the camel's back. The straw that sets you free to run away from Maya and to start looking at things for yourself!

"But the point I want people to understand first is that they need to drop everything, stop what they're doing and listen. Just shut up for a moment and bring everything back down to earth. I like to connect it to yoga with my clients. Breathe. It always starts with the breath. There's a domino effect from breathing properly. You can take back control just by starting to learn how to breathe."

"I imagine it can be quite confronting for a client if s/he summons the courage to say *Okay, I want to wake up* and then you say *Great! Drop everything you know!*"

I laugh, remembering the few times I've said it to people.

Sandra continues, "I mean, even if people can drop everything – including their concept about what it means to drop something – and step into nothing, then what? If you really get rid of everything, you're throwing your ideas and ideals, along with your version of reality, out of the window. What happens next? Is there a moment where you literally just step into nothingness?"

"That comes much later. But that's another of the things I was trying to say at the beginning about what people expect from the waking up process. People have this notion about what it means to be awake. They think it's nirvana, bliss, peace with the world – but it's not like that. When you get here, once you actually open your eyes, there's nothing. And that's significant because that very fact shines a light on all of the things that you let consume you and take your energy, your life and to affect you emotionally. They aren't real either, so they aren't relevant. They don't exist in themselves. Only your belief in them exists."

"And the value you place on that," Sandra says.

"Yes. Emotions confuse truth because emotion makes false values even stronger. Emotion feeds attachment. The stronger the emotion, the more likely it is that you are going underground. You aren't coming to the surface, you aren't waking up. You're just burying your head deeper under the sand."

Sandra bites her lip. "There's something about that step into nothingness, that idea of leaving everything you know behind, which is actually quite terrifying."

"Extremely terrifying! I went through a deep depression when I got to that point. Another part of your False Self dies off."

"So where does someone find the courage to go through with this?"

"For me, I wanted to know what was true and what was real. There are phases. Something will push you to focus on one concept until you reach a point of realization, understanding, destruction of that concept. Then your need to know everything about it falls away, and with it goes another small piece of your False Self. Once you settle into that new space of realization, something else will present itself, usually with another question. You keep going until you have no more questions."

"Which is why you put the emphasis on questions in your 200 hour intensive yoga course."

"Yes. The 200 hour yoga intensive gives people a structure to strengthen their personal practice. We meet every other month for a weekend of group practice and discussion and, in the months we don't meet as a group, we meet one-on-one. I remember wanting to cancel one weekend because when we met, no one had questions they were willing to discuss with the group. You either want this or you don't. If you don't have a question for a course that you are taking to deepen your practice, how can you expect to have a question to drive your own platform of thought forward? You need a question in order to answer it. Think about Gestalt therapy, for example. When you go and sit in front of a therapist, the therapist asks you *What's your question?* When your question is answered that period of therapy is done. It can take two weeks or it can take five years. It's pretty much the same with the intensive yoga course. And pretty much the same with the awakening process. You need to be actively focused on your question."

"So, in terms of the fire we spoke of earlier, it can be as simple as asking a question and getting an answer? How do you go from not being happy in your normal life and suspecting that there is something out there that you can't quite find, to a state of realization?"

"Something will trigger you. And that trigger will be different for every single person. But something will trigger you and it will awaken an unhappiness in you that you've been running from the whole time."

"Unhappiness? What do you mean by *unhappiness?*"

"Feeling like this is not my life. This cannot be my life."

"That it's somehow not enough?"

I nod. "That there's something missing. I hear it from students all the time. They say something is missing but they don't know what it is. That's when I tell them that they need to be silent. To listen. To start paying attention. It helps to shift your focus from what's *missing* to actually what's *not working* because that tells you what's holding you back. Is it a relationship, work, family issues? Whatever it is, drop it all and come to nothing within yourself. And then, listen. Find the crack in your reality that doesn't make sense and stare at it!"

"So, *coming to nothing* can simply be letting go of everything that you have attachments to. It's not necessarily stepping out into the oblivion of space?"

"Well, it's definitely not going outward because there is nothing out there. It's all inward – so you have to let go of all concepts of attachment to emotional, energetic and physical things. It's the only way to come back to what you know – which is nothing. And listen."

"And what are we listening for?"

"Nothing in the beginning. First, just try to enjoy the space, the emptiness. Once your mind is subdued you will begin to feel/connect with the True Self."

"And in that space the question arises?"

"Something can come out. And that something will be what's missing. You feel it inside of you. *This is fucked. I have a good job, I have a nice relationship, I have a nice everything but I'm not happy. Why am I not happy? What is this? If all of these things that I thought could make me happy, don't, then what?*

"The tendency," I continue, "is to go out. Always out, out, out, out, out... But nothing outside of you is real, so you're chasing your happiness within the realms of False Reality. That idea of the person you are longing to be doesn't exist. And the hardest part, really, is letting that go because then you don't exist anymore, either. We define ourselves by our ego and by our emotional connections to things that aren't true. That's how we define who we are and what we project onto the world. When you get to the point where you realize that the world as you know it doesn't even exist, you can't care about those things anymore? The question to ask then is *Why do I want to be connected to this? How is it serving me?* And that's where I'm trying to get my students. I'm trying to guide them to a place where they can actually find out what is missing. But you're not going to find it if you don't listen. And no one is really listening all the time. But that's how it starts."

I smile. "But, funnily enough, once you start to listen, you realize that nothing is missing. You're just lost in the idea of Self. Your False Self. And you eventually get to a point where all concepts of Self fall away, and when that happens, you listen and you are only listening to Atman."

Sandra sighs. "It sounds hard."

"I know. The end result seems so bleak, you might even wonder why it's worth going there at all."

"Yes," she says. "Why bother?"

"Bother because you want to be free from the weight and struggle that comes with keeping up the facade, the ego, the False Self. Bother because once you get here, it's total freedom."

"Yes." She nods, relieved.

"Just remember that this is only one step in the process of awakening, and it's really the hardest one I, myself, have faced so far."

"Do you think it's over, now? That you've arrived at a place where you'll stay?"

I laugh. "No! I'm pretty sure I have more to face, but everything I've experienced prior to the removal of that particular piece of Self wasn't as intense."

Death of the old Self

"There is no fundamental difference between
the preparation for death and the practice of dying,
and spiritual practice leading to enlightenment."
- *Stanislov Grof, psychiatrist*

Sandra and I are meeting again, only this time it's on a
different day of the week, at a different location and time and
the energy of our meeting is quite different, too.

"So, tell me, why are you here?" she asks with a smile.

"Something really strange has happened," I begin.

She raises an eyebrow.

"I guess you've been hearing that from me quite a lot, these days."

We both laugh.

I continue. "This time it's big. Really, really BIG. You know, when you want to think about something, you go to this place in your mind where you think or reflect or surrender to all the ideas you have? It's not that it's a separate part of you, exactly, but, in a way, it is."

She looks a little lost.

"Does that make sense? Like you have a special place in your mind where you go to think, to reflect, to remember?"

"A place where, maybe, you are a bit more in line with what you are, and a little less in the world?" she asks.

"Yes, the place where you separate mentally from your physical body.`'

She nods.

"There's nothing there anymore."

She blinks, not sure what to say. "Well, what used to be there?"

"Everything! My thoughts, ideas, emotions. My history. My past. EVERYTHING! It's that place where I go to dig around in my thoughts, concepts, ideas and feelings."

"Sounds like the place most people go when they are trying to meditate."

I smile. "Like a garage filled with all our old shit. That place we all have. That's where everybody goes to reflect on the things they are holding on to. Some people might see it as a garage. Some people might see it as a temple, a notebook, whatever. Well, mine is EMPTY! It used to be full and now EVERYTHING has GONE!"

"Oh!" She looks confused. "And, how does that feel?"

"Fucked up!"

"It feels fucked up? Doesn't it feel liberating?"

"Oh, yes, amazing! I mean "fucked up" in a very positive way. I've never felt so light. I'm vibrating. I'm flying! I'm completely energized all the time unless my body says *STOP! You need to stop.* My vibration is higher than ever and I feel free!

"I didn't expect this! I didn't expect this writing project to affect my own awakening process, either. I never thought I was fully awake, just that I was on the right track. That I was taking the steps, seeing the changes, doing the work. But this… this is surreal. We talked about it before, remember? That when you remove a piece of yourself and take time to settle into that new reality, then something else comes up."

She nods.

"Well, this time, nothing else came up. Nothing else is left. Nothing else is there. And that's the hardest part to explain. It's empty."

"What, exactly, was there before?" Sandra asks.

"It was a space full of feelings, ideas, my personality,

my life, my past. All the things that created my False Self and how I connected that False Self to this False Reality. Those things that are always there, neatly compartmentalized for you to go back and process. You know, the baggage we carry. We all have it and it's always there when you try to go and think. But now, there is nothing. It's empty."

"Blank? Like it was on that beach when the Maya wallpaper came down?"

"Exactly. That is now my conscious reality – and it makes me feel like I'm flying, in the sense that my vibration is so high."

"You released a lot of old stuff?"

"Destroyed it! Without doing anything other than changing my perspective." I pause, letting the impact of that sink in. "It's affecting everything. It's impacted my daily life – my basic interactions, my relationship, how I work, what I'm doing. If it wasn't one of the final steps in the process of awakening, it was the biggest one I have taken so far."

She leans forward, hesitant. "How has that affected the reality that you created around the character that we all knew as Jason. How has that changed?"

"I want to kill it."

"Kill it?" she asks. "So violently?"

"Yes."

...

"Do you think the emptiness is a temporary state? That you are moving from an old self into something you are creating but have not created yet?" Sandra asks.

"That's exactly what I think, and the step I just took and the piece that I have removed is either the final piece or the biggest piece yet. There's nothing left in that garage – because that all existed in the context of Maya. I've never had this much energy. Even when I was young I never remember having this much energy."

"A lightening up, then. An En-lightening!"

I can see my crazy is contagious as there's excitement in her eyes now, too.

"I'm sleeping less than I've ever slept," I continue. "My language is changing and my voice is changing – it's getting louder and it's getting more clear. I'm also writing more.

"Things are changing. I'm changing. My former identity, the character, Jason, as the world and I used to know him, is dead. Only the consciousness that animated him remains – and, in that consciousness, the awareness of what I want to do now."

Sandra leans in. "Which is?"

"Work with people who are serious about waking up. One-on-one. Even if they just want to wake up in their own life, right now."

"It's a good thing your old character, Jason, put Gianuario in charge of managing the yoga studios before you killed him off," she jokes.

I dropped the day-to-day running of the yoga studios eighteen months ago and left it completely in Gianuario's hands. He decided to stay on as manager once I came back from the ashram in France. While I was away, I realized that, although I thought I had created the life I wanted, it was too all consuming. I was trapped under the financial pressure of keeping a business running, and that stopped me from connecting to who I was and what I wanted to be. Leaving the studios in the hands of someone else, who I trusted and who had total freedom to do with them as he wished, was the action I needed to truly show the universe I was tired of fighting. I surrendered. I gave my life to the flow and stopped doing anything. Coming back to life as I knew it after my time away was extremely difficult because it no longer felt real to me. I made a deal with the universe that if it wanted me to have this business and this life, that it had to take over and make it happen. And it did.

"The old self and the life it was living, died. I destroyed it," I say.

She's watching me, carefully. "Did you need to destroy it?" she asks. "Couldn't it just have fallen away when the time was right? It can take a lot of energy to destroy something that can crumble away on its own."

"I don't mean destroy it in the sense of killing it off or dismantling it. I just mean I destroyed the part of myself that was attached to it. I fully removed myself from it and any outcomes associated with it."

"More like shedding a skin, then?" she suggests.

"Yes."

"Active but not necessarily violent." She exhales, more comfortable with that idea.

I nod.

"Letting go could even be an easy transformation," she ventures.

"Could be, but it usually isn't because of all our attachments."

We laugh.

"I just wanted it off me!" I say. "Like a pair of shoes that are a size too small."

Sandra frowns. "But how does that affect your intimate relationships? Your close friends, your partner, your dogs, even? You're changing. Your vibration has completely changed, so what happens to all the people who were connected with the old you at an intimate level?"

I take a moment to think. "Well, Gianuario, my partner, has been checking that it's not him. He keeps making jokes about it. For example, yesterday I spent the whole day out of the house, 12 hours straight, running errands and writing. I'm very focused on this process and I'm also trying to get rid of all the things that my previous self was responsible for that I don't want to do anymore. When I came home he asked very lightly, *You're not avoiding me, are you?* I sat him down and told him that he is the only person I could be going through this with. He might not be where I'm at at the moment, but he can understand (in some way) what I'm going through and what I'm talking about. But, as I told him, he has to understand that this process is nothing personal – nothing about him. I don't know what's happening, how it's happening or what will happen next. But I know we are supposed to be going through this together."

"What about your friends?"

"When I see friends now, and it's happened to me twice in one week, I am a bit disconnected. It's like *Hmm, what am I doing? Why am I talking to you? It's okay, but I'm not getting anything from this conversation and it seems like I'm wasting an opportunity or time or something.* And that was somebody that I have known for a very long time.

"I have another close friend who is on the same path – we've read books from the same teachers and use the same language to talk about how we understand the world. In fact, she's one of two people I can talk to who really understands every word I'm saying and can come back to me using the same language. But since this has happened, even that connection has gone."

"Sounds a little lonely," Sandra says. "But might it be that you made a jump and you're still finding your feet in the place where you landed?"

"That's what I was trying to discuss with her. I was asking for help. For insight. I wanted to know if I crossed a big fucking line or if I was just settling into a new way of being – because sometimes I don't know. She suggested I give it two weeks and then meet up again and talk. So you see, everything, every connection I had with everyone has changed, is still changing, and when I reach out, it's like there's nothing there. Nothing at all."

"But that nothingness brings a sense of elation with it, doesn't it? A sense of freedom?"

"Oh fuck, YES! That's why I'm vibrating. I can't be still. I'm flying inside. I really am and it's affecting my visual spectrum again. Even that is changing. My life was already two dimensional but even that doesn't look real, anymore. I can't relate to life as I knew it. It's becoming more difficult. It's like I know that you are here but I don't think that you are. I see you but I honestly think that you are just a figment of my process."

"You know, there are some psychologists out there who would say what you are describing is a sign of dissociation from the real world, and that you are dissociating because you can't deal with what you are facing in it."

"If Maya is what they like to call the real world then I see no problem with that."

"The outside world has become a projection?"

"Completely."

"And you are totally aware of that projection?"

"I really see it as only that. And it's okay, especially now that I have no more concern for human relationships."

She frowns. "No concern for human relationships at all?"

"I still find them entertaining and they need to stay entertaining, otherwise I'm going to get bored. So either I need to be entertained by relationships or they need to serve my process. Otherwise I don't see them lasting long."

Sandra frowns. "What do you mean by entertaining?"

"There being a mutual exchange/growth relationship. The relationship showing me another side of Maya that makes me laugh, or me showing them why I'm laughing."

"How did you see relationships before?"

"I saw them as fun – a way of developing the False Self, growing together, bouncing ideas and emotions off of each other, sharing life experiences together and things like that. But those are all things that happen inside the False Reality. They are all simply reflections of Maya – and that's no longer important to me. It's no longer my world. I live in a new place. And I want the relationships I have around me to reflect that."

"The way you describe that new place is very empty."

"Completely."

"But you find the emptiness quite beautiful – so it's like a kind of potential."

"It is. But I still have to find a way to make it work because this is where my body is until it dies. I can't live in nothingness forever so I'm trying to reshape my False Reality so that it accommodates me better."

"What do you mean? How can it accommodate you better?"

I have to think about that.

"Is it about the quality of the people who come across your path, the interactions you have?" she suggests.

"No, no... It's more like what I tell students when they start with me. *Get rid of the things that don't serve you!* So, now, I'm cleaning house but I'm cleaning house from a different realm."

"Not the realm of bricks and mortar..."

"No, I want to be rid of all that. Just like I want to be rid of my old character's role and identity. When I did go back to talk to my friend who is on the same spiritual path, we started laughing about this whole change of character business because I'm not anything anymore. And now that I'm nothing, I'm trying to find a voice to communicate something I've learned from becoming nothing." I laugh at the absurdity of it. "I feel like I've crossed into a new realm and I'm trying to find a way to communicate that back to everyone I left in the old one."

Sandra's still watching me carefully. "Part of the process seems to be the awareness of identity as expressed through a consciously chosen character. When we started talking, you said that you wanted to shift your character (again) and move away from the one you had just created with a turban and a big beard."

I laugh. "Yes. That character feels like he lived a long time ago..."

"Even then you were playing with the notion of a

character, anyone's character, being fluid, and also the notion of how a character you choose to embody affects how you are perceived and the relationships that develop from that. At the time, I remember you telling me it was immensely freeing not to be attached to the character you embodied, but to play with it, consciously. Now, it feels like you have dropped all of that and are reaching beyond character to the True Self, or something."

"Yes, that's why we are here. We are trying to find the essence of this experience, this process. We are trying to work out what is important so we can share it with other people."

"Teach them how to kill off their old characters, you mean?" She laughs.

"Yes. Because I do feel dead inside – but in a very positive way!" I can't say that without a smile on my face.

"Dead, meaning what? Complete?"

"No, my old self no longer exists. You see him because that's the person you know and relate to through my physical body and through our interactions and experiences. But I don't relate to him at all anymore."

Run

"One does not become enlightened by imagining
figures of light, but by making the darkness conscious.
The latter procedure, however, is disagreeable
and therefore not popular."
- C.G. *Jung, psychoanalyst*

"One of the things I've been interested in from the beginning of our conversation is your view of emotion," Sandra says. "The idea of emotion being linked to drama and it basically being a distraction from what's really going on."

I nod.

"So I was wondering about emotional qualities – like compassion, humility or patience. Where do those fit in from the perspective you have now? What are they?"

"My first instinct is that they don't exist because they are human emotions and I don't feel human anymore."

She raises an eyebrow. "Not human? But what, then? Are you stone? Elemental?"

"Am I stoned?" I laugh. "Like did I just smoke a joint?"

"Not stoned, stone. Like an element – star or stone. Or are you a vague space of potential?"

"I'm just aware. Conscious."

"Just consciousness?"

"Consciousness and energy. That's it."

"So, when you look out there," she gestures to the busy street outside. "What do you see? Do you see the cars or do you go beyond the objects to the movement everything is making?"

I stare out the window. "It looks like a screen. I know it's completely illusory."

"Can you cut through the screen?"

"Of course. And if I do it's the emptiness I go to when I think. The same thing I saw when the sky collapsed, when Maya revealed herself. Behind all that," I point out the window, "is emptiness."

"What about those moments you've talked about like 'your' dog approaching you on the street?"

"The sparkling?"

"Yes. What's that, then? In the nothingness behind the screen is there still light?"

"That's all energy within Maya."

"Do you think energy has a form – like water or something?"

"Yes, and I see that form in the patterns of the universe and sometimes visually like the day that I found Gumbo."

"What about your other senses? Hearing or taste. Do you still taste?"

"I still enjoy the sensory world very much. I still enjoy sex, food and alcohol. I like all of those things because what else is there to like when you no longer feel a connection to the False Self? I'm still here and I'll be staying here, in this world, for a while. It's going to get very boring if I don't, at least, enjoy my sensory experience. Right now, though, I'm very happy with my boredom."

"But that's what I'm wondering. That's my original question. Why are you here today? Now? In this altered state?"

"In the grand scheme of things I am here for this project. That's why I'm here. In my opinion, I'm here because I have a voice for something that I don't understand yet, and for something I've been trying to look for since I can remember. I've always looked for answers and truth. For me, I was always searching for enlightenment. I wanted to really be awake and aware. That was always my goal and I never thought I would find it. Ever. So in a way, I gave up looking – at least on the outside. But in that giving up, I started digging deeper on the inside. And look what I found..." I laugh. "Nothingness. But in that nothingness I know my True Self and I see my False Self. The False Self is me, the character, the person you see here in front of you. I see him, too, but the True Self and the False Self are two separate things."

"Connected, somehow."

"Sharing bodies, if you will. If that makes sense. I don't feel I control who you see – the Jason you know. I have no control over what he does and what goes on.

"It's really like I'm watching everything unfold, but the control of how that happens is with my True Self. That's where I can influence things by having scope of vision and changing my actions mentally based on that."

"So, the Jason I see is an interaction of my dream and of you activating your False Self on the edge of my dream?"

"Well, yes, if you are even here..."

We laugh.

"But we don't know for sure, do we?" I ask. I'm really having fun with this. "We really don't. I'm just aware of what's going on around me. That's the funny thing about waking up – it's nothing, which is exactly the opposite of Maya, which is our obsession with everything. And that everything is what distracts you from the nothingness, which is truth. Maya and attachment to Maya, is the source of depression, anxiety and suffering."

"Say that again..."

We can't stop laughing.

"That's really important but say it again. Can you even say it again?"

"I don't know! Sometimes this shit just comes out of me."

"I was just kind of like.. *Whoa, wait a minute! I missed a step there.*"

"Let me try." I swallow. "Where I am there is nothing."

She nods.

"But human obsession is about everything except that nothingness. And the *everything* humans are so concerned with, is only layers of Maya – distraction from the nothingness that is actual existence.

"Suffering, trauma, all of these things take place in the layers of distraction of Maya. This is even more proof that none of it is real because there is nothing left in the garage that was my storage space. Any part of my old self that I could connect to, relate to, bond with or reflect on is now gone. Gone."

"Are you saying suffering and trauma are illusions?" she asks.

"Yes, in the same sense that everything is an illusion."

"You know, the way you describe the state you have been in with the revelation of Maya and everything falling away as being alone on a rock hurtling through space, isn't a very attractive vision."

"It's not very attractive, Sandra, that's the point. It's not very attractive at all, but it's the truth."

"So what I keep coming back to is *Why wake up?* If you can master the dream, and it's a better dream than hurtling through space alone, why leave it?"

"One of my favorite writers, Jed McKenna, asks himself the same question. He says what most people who seek enlightenment really want is to just be awake within False Reality. You can have a good time there. But when you get this far in the process of awakening, there is nothing. And, there's no going back, either. I wouldn't want it any other way, myself. That's why I ask at the beginning of my work with students, *What do you want?* Now that I'm going through this process myself, when someone comes to me for coaching I can know from them, I can feel in them, whether they just want to be a bit more awake in their own life or if they want to be removed from it and enlightened." I laugh. "Enlightened, or whatever you want to call it. I hate that word because of the stigma around it, the false definition. People think enlightenment is a union with God, with everything, the universe, the world and all humanity but that's simply not true. All of those things exist within you as emotional constructs of Maya. Everything about that definition of enlightenment is not of the True Self. Enlightenment is a full removal of the veil that is Maya, not a new direction to explore within it."

"There's this great novel by Milan Kundera called *The Unbearable Lightness of Being* and every time you say "enlightenment" that's what I get a sense of. An incredible freedom of just being."

"That's exactly where you end up."

"If you're not afraid," she says, quickly. "I imagine there's a huge fear that comes with taking a decision to walk into the nothingness of freedom."

"Fear stops you from all sorts of things. That's just one of Maya's biggest fucking fish hooks... like *RRRAAARRRRRGGGGGHHHHH*. She just puts it in you – Fear – like a grappling hook. She's always got you with fear."

"How do you unhook? How do you stop being afraid?"

"I've always run at it. My whole life. When I was afraid of something, I questioned why I was afraid of it and then I made myself do it. Run at it. Run towards it screaming and wielding a knife. Even going to India to start studying yoga the first time when I was 23. I have never liked flying. It feels unnatural being hurtled through space in an aluminum tube."

"With a bunch of people you don't know..."

"Exactly, 30,000 feet above the earth, fighting its gravitational pull. Like *Hey, what are we doing up here?* It's always felt unnatural. When I started looking for places to do my first yoga course, the one that I connected with the most was actually the one that was the farthest away from me. That's another one of the reasons I chose it. I had to spend 22 hours in the air just to get there."

"Where was it?"

"Very deep in the south of India, the most southern tip. At the time I was living in San Francisco. So San Francisco to Seoul, Seoul to Bangkok, Bangkok to Chennai and then Chennai to Trivandrum. 22 hours in the air and I thought, *Okay, let's do it! You're afraid of flying, fucking go for it!* What happened? Nothing.

"That's how you confront fear, and that's also how you have to confront life. Death needs to be present, in your face, like a ticking clock, otherwise what's your motivation to do anything? There's always tomorrow. No! All of this could be over tomorrow. My fear of flying was connected to dying and death – as with most people who are afraid of flying. It's because they don't want to die because then the ego is gone. So I confronted that fear and the others that came up along the way.

"That's what you have to do with fear. It's the only way to deal with it. Pick up the knife and run!"

...

"I'm wondering," Sandra says, "how to take people from the idea of fear as terrifying limitation into the idea of the potential fun that you can have with it."

"If people really knew what enlightenment was, I'm not sure they would want it at all!" I laugh. "They would be a lot more interested in having fun right here."

"Being awake in the False Reality?" she asks.

I nod.

"It's totally possible and it could be fun, right?" She asks. "So how do you take people from a fear of losing what they have, into an understanding of the freedom that you gain by losing your previous confinement? For example, when people lose their jobs or finally get out of a destructive relationship, they don't usually run about saying *Oh, great – I'm free!*"

"No, they usually jump straight back into something similar."

"They go into panic, *Oh, my God! Now what? I don't want to deal with this!* So how do you take them from that fear of freedom to seeing the fun of freedom? The potential you have to create whatever you want?"

"It's very individual. And it's something I like to work with one-on-one with people."

"I think there is a line," Sandra says. "I think fear and freedom border each other."

"Yes, but the thing is if you cross it, you fall back. I'm just as guilty. It happened to me a lot. I'm not afraid of anything, anymore, but I used to be. And crossing that line and falling back again used to happen all the time as a result. Even with opening my business. I was afraid that if I become completely self employed I would be bound to an overhead of rent, insurance, staff – and I might not make it. But I went ahead and did it, anyway. What was the worst thing that could happen? There is no worst that can happen because I'm going to die, and who cares if I die in debt or not? I don't care about these things anymore. I really don't." I laugh. "I suppose, as I just turned 40, this could also be my version of a mid-life crisis."

She laughs.

"But taking all of the spirituality and awakening process out of what I'm saying, it could simply be that I'm done doing things that don't serve me."

"Maybe a mid-life crisis is really an opportunity to come back to the idea of what it is you want to do here..." she suggests.

"Yeah, what the fuck do you want?"

"Why are you here?"

"Right!"

She looks out the window at the busy roundabout, quiet for a moment. "And maybe that question echoes through our lives. You know, we come up with some notion of what we are going to do with our life, and then we forget. And we know, somewhere, that we have forgotten, so we spend the rest of our lives trying to remember what it was we wanted in the first place."

"Or, you can just shake off all of the bullshit around you. That's what I'm trying to do with the students on my course. They don't know it yet but I'm going to share this experience with them soon. I haven't decided when, yet, but I'm gonna throw it at them and see how it goes over." I smile at the thought. "Some of them are slowly becoming aware of where I'm at and what's going on. We have an email thread that we share, where we talk to each other. One of my students completely removed herself from all social media so we have to use email and I respect that – so we are going old school."

Sandra smiles. "Email is not so old school!"

"I know, but now it is – and we're older, so it's just school, I guess."

Another long laugh.

"But every now and then I read things that are happening to them and it confirms that teaching a course like this is helping me find the right voice to describe this process.

"And, that's what I want to do – work with people in groups, one-on-one, whatever, and share this process. Not because I want to wake them up, but because I want them to fucking chill out and enjoy their lives. Life is so brief and so unimportant in the end. If you don't enjoy it – it's really nothing at all. By running towards your fears you are confronting the ego, head on. If people can force themselves to do it, just once, they can begin the process. It takes only one huge leap or act to show the universe that you are ready for change to begin.

It's the same but different

"Enlightenment must come little by little,
otherwise it would overwhelm."
- *Idries Shah, author*

"How are you feeling?" Sandra asks. It's been a couple
of weeks since we last met. "You were on this great high the
last time we spoke and then you crashed."

"Yes, my body crashed and I slept. Hard. For two days I was useless. It's cool, though, because my perception is still completely changed. I just used up all of my energy. I don't know if it was excitement or processing or what. I don't know, but I've really been dead."

"Dead?" she raises her eyebrows.

"Physically speaking, yes. Exhausted."

"Some traditions talk about epiphanies or spiritual insights as being the release of stagnant energy which allows you to flow into a new level of understanding. In that sense your awakening freed up a lot of energy. Maybe you've been over buoyant for a while, and have now come back down to a more normal level of energy. This might seem like a collapse because you've been on an artificial high."

"So my natural state is tired? That's what you're telling me?" I laugh.

"Your energy level is a lot lower than it was the last time I saw you. Let's just leave it like that."

I find this to be a perfect segway. "An old friend recently called me out of the blue for an impromptu visit. She's a yoga teacher and on her own journey, as well. She's trying to 'wake up.' I only got to see her for 35 minutes before she left for the airport but it was interesting because she's having similar experiences right now. As I started to describe what had happened to me with Maya last year she cut me off and continued the sentence – because she had the same exact experience in her own process. Only difference was that her vision/perception didn't stick. She had an awakening but the impact of that is not a constant. With me, now, everything I see is Maya. It's clear as crystal."

"Why do you think that is? That the changed perception sticks with some people but not with others?"

"I don't know. It could just be that she's still breaking through more things. I guess it didn't really stick for me when it happened the first time, either. It threw me for a loop but it resonated as if I had only *seen* the concept. It didn't really affect my full vision while I was processing. It was as if I stepped away from it to allow the processing to happen." I think for a moment. "As I said before, I have to do everything at least twice to get it right. Maybe the same thing is to be said for visualizations linked to Maya."

Sandra frowns. "You just talked about visualization, and visualization is something different from a vision. Are you making that distinction or not? A vision seems to come from outside and appears before you. It has its own life. Whereas a visualization, for me, at least, is where you think about creating something visual in your mind and exploring it. You are the one generating it."

"I'm talking in the language of my new visual spectrum. A visualization is combined with a deep understanding, a paradigm shift in my mind. It's like a punch to my brain, my consciousness – whatever you want to call it. As I get a sensation, I have a specific thought, and, at the same time, I get a vision and my brain finally understands what it is I have been focusing on. The breakthrough, if you will.

"I'm a very visual person so my thought processes are visual, too. For example, when I first had a vision of consciousness, I think I drew it for you. The vision of Maya was similar because that's what was holding all consciousness in one place - like a layer around all things known. As I did that initial drawing, I remember little pieces would pop out."

"Pop out?" Sandra asks. "How?"

"Pop out like strong bursts shooting out away from the center only to be pulled back in. Waking up is your little piece popping out and breaking through Maya so that you can actually turn around and observe everything, consciously."

We contemplate my scribble for a moment.

"That's my visual spectrum," I continue. "That's how I see Maya and consciousness completely intertwined. Maya is like a sheath over reality – and that makes perfect sense to me now. But only because I've experienced it, and have seen it with my own eyes or mind. With my, whatever you want to call it, my vision." I laugh. "Actually, I don't know what to call it yet..."

"You said your vision, or your consciousness, punched through the sheath that is Maya so you could turn back and observe."

I nod.

"So, from where you are now, you're back to looking.

There is a sense of observing and looking as opposed to acting. Is that right?"

"Life, now, is like watching a show. I'm the spectator and the show is my life. I see the character Jason but I am no longer him."

"And if you want something to happen, say, this book to develop. Then you just..." She struggles to find words, then shrugs. "Well, what do you do?"

"My wants are not like that. I don't have big wants. It's more that I've become so present and aware of what's going on around me that I sort of see where things are going and just encourage them. The book we are working on is not a huge *I want this*. No. It started to unfold and I kept following the trail."

"So in a sense, that state of observation is a state of equanimity or something. There is no positive desire one way or the other. There is just a *Oh, let's see what this does* or *Oh, that pathway is lighting up*. Like a game, almost."

"Exactly! That's exactly what it is and you can play along. When you fight back or try to control it, everything stops. If you have egotistical wants like material things, it's not like you can just make those things happen. But my wants are in the trajectory of where I see my life going, so I try to fine tune it along the way. Encourage it to keep going – a little push, here, a little follow-up, there."

"And that trajectory, is that like your spiritual path, your destiny or your karma? Do you see it like that? Or is it just where you are and what's unfolding as you become aware of it?"

"I, personally, don't believe in karma anymore. I did but the more I'm having this experience the more I realize that it's like an excuse for something happening. Karma only exists as as an idea to help you reflect on where you are and how you got there."

"Going back to this notion of the trajectory of your life," Sandra says. "So it's not karma, not a spiritual path, not destiny or soul learning? Do any of those ideas even resonate with you, now? Do you work with any of those as concepts?"

"No."

We laugh.

"Okay," she continues, "because what I come back to often in our conversations is this idea of waking up and realizing you're all alone on a rock hurtling through space. If that's the case, if there is no reason for that, no bigger picture, then there's no reason to do anything or to not do anything. There's no reason to even continue."

"Some people have this sort of awakening experience and then they just go back to how they were before."

"Well, they probably go back to life as they knew it because it's pretty confronting," she says. "I mean, what do you do with a vision of reality, like that? That's my question. If you're sitting on your rock hurtling through space on your own, why are you there? Why are you here? I don't know."

"I don't, either." I laugh. "All I know is that I'm

conscious of this experience. I don't know why."

Sandra bites her lip. She's not sure about this.

"And who wants to know, anyway?" I say. "The False Self? It doesn't exist. If the False Self wants to know something, it is to have one more thing to hold on to, because that will make it seem more real."

"Doesn't that depress you?" Sandra asks.

"When I had my first really powerful realization of *You are alone in every sort of way you can grasp loneliness. This is a solo experience. Completely, completely solo!* I got very depressed. A lot of us rely on human relationships, emotion and contact to keep us up, to keep us going, to give us something to live for. When you realize that you are actually alone, it's tough. All that we thought we were living for is only energy flowing. People represent different spectrums of that energetic flow.

"In fact, I fell into a deep depression – but not for long, only a couple of weeks. But during that time I didn't leave the house. I was like *What's the fucking point?* But the reality of the situation is that even when you get that far in your realization process, you're still here – and there is nothing you can do about it. So, if you are planning to stick around, you have to settle back in."

Sandra sighs. "In some of the traditions I've worked with, if you have any sort of mental instability – if you're on medication or you've had heavy hallucinogenic experiences, they won't touch you. They say that you are already unstable, and if they take you any further down their path, you're likely to become more so as you realize everything you thought was real, solid and that you could rely on, isn't that way at all. By implication, any sense of awakening to the truth, to a greater reality, can lead to implosion, annihilation, self destruction. The way you describe your awakening process seems to echo the idea that we, as humans, are not so well equipped to handle the nature of reality. So what I'm wondering is, what drives us? What drives the will to continue living in the face of understanding that there is no point to it?"

I have to think that over. Sometimes I can feel an answer is coming – the gears are turning, but I don't know how long it will take for the words to form. At other times, answers come like a flow of running water.

"It's a big question," she says, smiling. "You don't have to answer it right now."

"No, no...I'm processing. Sometimes I have to wait and let things settle. To see. Why is it like this with humans? I don't know. A dog never questions its nature. Animals never question their nature. At least, not as far as we know!"

"They don't generally commit suicide."

"Dolphins, do," I say. "And sometimes in groups."

"Do they? How interesting! Well, most animals, as far as I know, rarely stop living by choice. Even in the most dire of circumstances they fight to survive. So, what makes us so different? And how much of that difference is linked to

Maya?" She thinks for a moment. "I'm also interested in what you were saying about relationships. It's true, life is a solo experience, but a lot of people are clinging to others because it makes it easier for them to continue or because they like it that way. But a lot of the drama that I see playing out in the lives of people who come into my practice is actually drama around other people. Their job is fine, their health is fine, things are fine. Then they get into conflict with someone else."

"Humans like drama. That's clear."

"Why is that?"

"Fear. Honestly, and I think I've said this before, I see fear in almost everybody's eyes. The more distracted people can become from the reality that our existence is ultimately meaningless, the easier it is."

"So that's it? We use all the drama as a distraction?"

"We feed fuel to the drama that is our life. That is Maya. Maya is drama."

"And drama has you pumped up on adrenaline and cortisone and if you are running on those stress hormones I'm wondering if you feel, temporarily, more alive. I'm starting to wonder how much drama is about distraction and how much it is a quest to feel more alive. For life to really matter for a moment?"

"It's both. If you are completely convinced that you and your ego are real, why would you go looking for something else?"

Leaving the show behind

"How could they see anything but the shadows
if they were never allowed to move their heads?"
- *Plato, The Allegory of the Cave*

"Do you feel any different this week?" Sandra asks, checking her notes. "We've missed a couple of weeks, haven't we?"

"Yeah, two weeks. One because I was dying, physically - and, spiritually, too, I guess. It's funny, this flu came at the perfect time. I had a whole week that I didn't leave the house and I was so sick I didn't feel anything. I was very empty. That emptiness really permeated my physical and mental being. I thought about, felt, sensed... nothing."

"And you were also alone, weren't you? Gianuario was away. It was just you and the dogs."

"Yes, and now I feel different." I laugh. "I'm not 100 percent, but maybe 90 percent and that's a very good thing. I was thinking about us meeting today while I was lying in bed this morning. I was asking myself *What do I feel?* And the answer is still nothing. I think it's permanent."

"Let's talk about that nothingness. What is it? There is a nothingness that borders on terror, like nihilism. And there's a nothingness where there is no need, no desire and no push to do anything. Which is it?"

"It's the second one. It's funny because I had a private session with one of the students on the course recently. I have them reading the *Bhagavad Gita*, and she was making comments about it and we ended up talking about family drama. That's one of the issues raised in the *Gita*. I told her what it means for me, in this state, not to have an emotional connection to my family and I described it to her. I can't remember the words I used so I won't try to recreate the conversation, but as I started to speak I could fear mounting in her eyes. People think if you sever the emotional ties to your family, you have nothing left in your life. All she could think about as we talked was her overwhelming fear of loneliness – that same loneliness which is, actually, the only truth. But then as I explained it to her from where I am now she said *You know, that sounds a lot better*."

Sandra sighs. "I think that's how most people are going to react to any sense of cutting family ties. One of the first reactions will be fear because we surround ourselves with people, things that keep us anchored in our daily world."

"It's all distraction," I say.

"Maybe, but family can also anchor us in a sense of continuity, of solidity, of familiarity and no change. And, this freedom, in the way you describe it, is all about change. I think that's why people find it so scary." She pauses, thinking. "So how did you change your expression of the idea of moving away from family ties and family drama from a way that frightened her to a way that seemed acceptable?"

"What made it acceptable was very simple. I said something like *I still love them. I still care about them as beings because we're all the same thing, anyway. And since I no longer connect with my physical body, my character or persona, because I know it's not who I am, I can't get involved with theirs, because I know it's not who they are.*'"

"You can't get involved, or you choose not to?"

"Both. I still care about them, of course, and I do love them – just in a different way. I was talking with a close family friend last week, Susan, and she was telling me about her usual life drama and because I didn't react to her stories by colluding with her or sympathizing, she asked if I was upset with her."

"You weren't playing with her. You weren't feeding that fire."

I nod. "I'm simply not getting involved. I said, 'No. I'm not upset with you, at all. I just don't care about those things anymore.' And she thought that was strange because her family is partially my family, too. Then, later on in the conversation I told her that it all sounded like the same bullshit over and over and over again, anyway."

"Sort of like, *If that's what you choose to do, that's fine. I love you. But I'm not feeding it.*"

I nod. "It's not that I don't want to hear about it, I'm just not involved so I can't give an emotional response because I don't have emotions attached to any of it.

"For instance, on a different day, I got a message about an aunt who is in the hospital. They don't know what happened, but one day she just couldn't stand up. Her heart was blocked and she needed bypass surgery. Four bypasses, it turned out! My stepmom was messaging me about it and I didn't know how to respond. I knew what my stepmom wanted, expected even, in terms of a response but I was not emotionally involved with my aunt or the surgery, so I wasn't in a space to do that authentically. On a personal level, my relationship with my aunt has always been complicated. On another level, the hospital drama is part of this whole character thing. I know she is not only that person undergoing surgery. She is much bigger than that. So, what do I say to my stepmom without sounding like a dick and still staying true to myself?"

"When you say she is bigger than the person undergoing surgery, are you referring to the separation between the physical vehicle of the body and consciousness that is embodied by it?"

"Yes. And that's a huge separation."

"And one is not the other but, in a sense, physical incarnation is dependent on the vehicle. So if the vehicle dies then that consciousness disappears or goes back to the source?"

"It goes back to Brahman, yes."

"So what you're saying is that your connection to people now is not as individuals, but as embodied expressions of the ultimate source."

"Embodied expressions of the whole. Yes."

"And that's how you're conducting your relationships on all levels at the moment?"

"I'm trying to, but in reality, I'm still sorting it out." I pause, remembering. "I didn't even respond to those messages about my aunt because I didn't know what to say without sounding like a soulless asshole. And that's how they would interpret it. I don't have this kind of emotional attachment, now, so I don't know how to communicate with people who do have them. Do I communicate intellectually or do I communicate from my new found self, my more realized, awakened perspective? I know what's right for me, but all they know is the life and death drama they live in. The daily circus of their lives. And I'm not sure they would appreciate me poking holes in it."

"The timing of this realization is interesting. It came just at the point where there was a break in the notion of family lineage or family connection in your processing. The garage of things still to process was empty. Everything you had stored there to go back to later, had gone. Then you went through this period of getting over the flu, or dying, or..."

"I was really dying!" I insist with a laugh.

She gives in, begrudgingly. "Okay, so last week you were dying, and the week you choose to resurrect yourself, you run straight into some serious family stuff."

"Right!"

"Is it normal to have that level of family drama in your life or was that excessive, even for your family?"

"With my family, and with that friend Susan, in particular, this high level of drama is very normal. There are always waves. It's seasonal or cyclical with her. Every three months some sort of drama consumes her life for a while. With her, that's okay."

I sigh. "With my aunt, it's different. I never hear anything from her or about her and I don't see her when I go home. I don't care about her ego/character in any way. She almost died, or they thought she was dying so they were just letting me know. I don't think I told my family explicitly that I didn't care, though."

"Which brings us to the question of acting on feeling and personal truth. How do you communicate in a way that is authentic to your new self and..."

"Not come across as a dick?" I joke.

I was going to say, not sound *unacceptable*, somehow." Sandra smiles. "Yes. It brings up two issues. One is that of social convention, because social convention governs how people react in certain situations – what we say, what we do. For instance, if someone is in the hospital dying, you let people know. It's convention – whether you care that it's the right thing to do, or not. So I wanted to ask you about the value of social convention."

"When you finally see everything as Maya and the concept of self disappears those things simply don't matter anymore. The False Self is absorbed in the drama of Maya, not the True Self. Now, after enlightenment, you need to settle back into the role of the character and rules of social convention help you to connect with other people and sound less detached. In that sense, I guess, it's helpful."

"I also wanted to ask about the other side of that. Which is where convention slips, which it quite often does, into sentimentality. What does sentimentality mean to you in your current state?"

"Sentimentality for whom? Me or the person who is communicating with me?"

"For the person communicating with you. I'm assuming you don't feel sentimental often."

"I still experience emotion so there can be sentimental feelings here and there, but in a joyful sense, not one of longing. But for the person I'm communicating with, well, as with all emotions that are guiding them, I try to help them see the source of that emotion so they can separate themselves from it. It doesn't matter what the emotion is – emotions are all kind of the same.

"Everybody's life is filled with issues, with drama, with ups and downs. Everybody has their shit. Everybody has their baggage. Sentimentality is a way of going back and candy coating the baggage. Of re-creating the situation and only taking the happy feelings from those periods and embracing them. That's why we like it so much. It's cherry picking the past and highlighting the good points. When I see someone doing that I ask *Why are you doing that?*"

"And nostalgia? Is that the same thing for you?"

"Well, nostalgia is bigger. Sentimentality is personal. Nostalgia is more general like the community you lived in, the school you went too or the time you lived in. Sentimentality is the song that was playing that day and how it resonated with you personally, then, and how it resonates now."

"A shortcut into hitting an emotional high from the past?"

"Yes. To me, again, you are reconnecting to an emotion that you had, and amplifying the good bits."

"One of the things that keeps coming up as we talk is the separation between feeling and intellect. You've done it a number of times and each time you've done it differently. That's what's interesting. You talked about lying in bed this morning and trying to work out what you felt. In a lot of new age thinking and spiritual thought it's all about feeling. Get your head out of the way and listen to your heart. But, just now, when you were talking about how to talk to your dad's wife or expressing how you feel about your aunt. You said you can't connect on that level."

"Yes. I don't connect on an emotional level."

"But you can express an emotional connection on an intellectual level."

"Yes."

"What I want to talk about is the difference between 'feeling' and 'emotion' and where the intellectual process comes in."

"Feeling and emotion are completely different things to me."

Sandra leans forward. "What is a feeling?"

"A feeling is something that I witness and observe that comes from my True Self."

"Inside you?"

"Inside me."

"It's a stimulus that you feel but that you are observing at the same time?"

"Yes."

"So, there's a bubbling sensation or tension..."

"No," I interrupt. "It's not a physical thing. It's energetic."

"For example, when you were getting all these texts from your stepmom, what sort of feeling was that? Frustration?"

"No, because that's an emotion."

"That's what I'm trying to get to. What is the difference between an emotion and the energetic expression of that emotion that you are calling a feeling?"

"An emotion is a response of the ego to the life of the character, Jason. When I say I feel something, that feeling is coming from a different place, from awareness itself, from being the constant observer of the flow around me. That's the energy I'm trying to speak of. Feelings are more like messages. Intuition."

"So, maybe, one is an extension of the other. A working out of a message that's not given clearly, understood or acted on. I wonder if that's what happens? You get a very clear feeling that something isn't right, but you keep doing it anyway. That feeling builds into something stronger because you haven't acted on it. So maybe that's where you get the emotion, be it anger, or resentment or guilt or whatever. You've gone down a path that's not right. If you could unravel the emotion, especially a negative emotion, maybe you could get back to the feeling?"

"Could be, because people never listen to their gut.

That's what I mean as a feeling. People talk of feeling things in their heart, in their bones, their gut. That's feeling. Your bones and your gut feel. They don't have emotions."

"So, feeling is a very physical thing."

"If you call energy physical. It's an energetic shift. And I guess you feel it inside you in a way that I don't see as physical, but you could call it that. Those are the things that I watch for. When I feel something, I observe it."

"That's kind of curious, isn't it?" She laughs. "Watching a feeling."

"Yes, but that's what I do. I ask what is it trying to tell me? What is this for? Those questions direct my attention to what is really happening."

"It's not watching as much as it is observing. Taking a stimulus from a realm of feeling into understanding." She muses.

"Into your intellect. Putting your intellectual light on it."

"So, how do you not over intellectualize? Isn't that the problem a lot of people have these days. They make feeling and emotion safe by keeping feeling in the grip of intellectualization?"

"Yes, which is why the title of this book is *Get Your Head Out of Your Asana*. I want people to understand that. I want people to look so closely at themselves that they begin to dissect who they really think they are. If you can destroy the connection that you have to just one emotion, you can begin the process of waking up."

"So there is no separation, really? It's not about getting the head out of the way. It's getting preconditioned responses to emotion out of the way?"

I pause a moment to think. "Sort of, but that's kind of doing it backwards. I don't think I can tell someone not to be an emotional being if they want to get to the awakened state. Not being emotional is just a side effect of this state, just as flexibility is a side effect of a regular yoga practice. That's one of the problems I have sometimes with spiritual books. They tell people to practice non-attachment, non-emotion. You can't tell someone living in fear in their False Reality to just stop! You can't just stop feeling the things you are feeling, because those things are part of the state you are living in. You have to get out of that state all together to really change things. It's more like changing your perspective. Completely."

"How does someone do that? Take someone who is very emotional, for example. Someone who is very wrapped up in fear, like the person you were talking about earlier. There is a fear of isolation and loneliness if they cut their existing ties to family. That can get very emotional, so where do you start?"

"First, I would have to ask them, *What do you want? Do you like this drama?* Some people do. Some people want it. They thrive on it. It makes them feel alive. My friend Susan will never admit it but she loves drama. She's helpless, for what I do."

"Meaning she doesn't want to change?"

"Yes, she doesn't want change. She likes the dynamic of the chaos with its ups and downs."

"She's riding the emotions, and enjoying it."

"Yes, that's all she is doing. She will say she's unhappy and say that she doesn't like it, but she won't make any changes to stop it happening. And sometimes she embraces situations that create even more drama when she doesn't have to. Her behavior shows me that she likes her life that way. Maybe, not all of it. Maybe, not all of the time. But enough of the time not to change."

Sandra looks out the window, watching streams of people on the street outside pass us by. She's silent for a minute. "So how and if you change your state depends on your answer to that question, *What do you want?* Do you want to be bound emotionally to your family? Do you want to be bound to the career you hate, the relationship that you're in that doesn't work? Whatever. First they have to make their decision, and then they can start the process of changing their lives to meet it."

"Yes. If a person were to come to me wanting to be free from, hypothetically speaking, family drama - if that's really how they wanted to start changing his or her life, I think the best thing someone can do in that situation is a hard cut. If they have close ties, they can just tell everyone that they are taking a month off. Disappearing. You start there, with action."

"Some of the practices I have worked with see words as energy. Usually, a waste of energy!" She laughs. "During the practice you are in a conscious retreat of silence. You talk as little as possible for a month. You don't initiate conversation or interaction and get out of interaction as quickly as possible if someone, anyone, initiates it with you."

"That sounds awesome!"

"It's really amazing because when you are consciously trying to preserve your words and only using 10 or so a day, you hear how people vent. When someone is going off at you and you don't respond, you actually realize there is no space to say anything, anyway. Not unless you are agreeing with them. When people are venting, they aren't listening. And if people aren't open to listening, there isn't much point using your words on them."

I nod. "Most people are talking only to talk. That's it. It really comes back to connecting to the True Self. Non-attachment is the result of it. You can't do it backwards. You can try. You can consciously fight not being attached, but it's hard when you don't really know what that means. And you don't truly understand non-attachment until you get here. Then, it changes everything!"

Why yoga?

"Everyone has a spirit that can be refined, a body that can be trained in some manner, a suitable path to follow. You are here to realize your inner divinity and manifest your innate enlightenment."
- *Morihei Ueshiba, martial artist*

"We talked about this being the anti-yoga yoga book," Sandra says, with a smile. "Or the yoga book that isn't. You've established a certain presence through the practice of yoga and what you're doing now is different from that, but wouldn't have necessarily come about without it. How do you connect the two? Where you are now and the path you took to get here?"

"That's a good question. If I had to say what tools from yoga helped me to get here, I'd have to say breath. That's where it all starts. It begins with proper breathing and that starts to change your physiology. In the end, choosing to be awake, to be enlightened, even, is about changing your intellectual sight. Your focus. You need to be focused on what you want – and be focused on that while living, eating, breathing – whatever it is that you want.

"I wanted to know the truth and that set my intent and focus. But the practice of yoga helps create this ability to focus. It helps you quiet your mind. It helps you direct your focus to one thing via breath and meditation.

I pause, thinking. "It also promotes harmony. If you're focusing on breathing and your breath is harmonized in the body, there is a unity. Some people are so busy in their minds, they forget to breathe at all, except in short, shallow gasps. You can't go inside, if you don't know where or what your body is.

"In yoga, we use the body to bring the focus inside. That's where all the answers are. Everything is right inside of you. I found nothing on the outside. Nothing at all."

"Is that where this idea of the physical vehicle comes from?" Sandra asks. "If we are all part of the great source why are we encapsulated off into separate, physical bodies."

"Experiences."

"So each individual and all he, or she, experiences is perfectly valid? Perfectly as valuable as anything else?"

I nod. "Completely. One person's life is as valuable as any other because it's another experience for consciousness, for Brahman, to have."

"So in terms of focus and yoga practice you can say that it doesn't matter what the focus is? You wanted to know the truth but someone else might want to–"

"Somebody might want to write an opera," I interrupt. "Yes – do it! But make sure that's what you really want. What you desire has to come from your True Self and not your ego. If it's an egoistic desire, it isn't going to work. For instance, it would be stupid for me to say that I want to win an Oscar. I'm not an artist, composer, screenwriter or actor. That would never happen because the desire of wanting to win an Oscar doesn't come from a pure state. If I said I would like this book to be written so that I can get this message out to people and help them, that's something that's a bit more real and in line with my life. As I focus everything on it and stay there, things fall into place and the book starts to manifest. Anyone can do that."

"How do you know if what you want is from a pure place? Some people may be less in tune with themselves and the nature of their true desires."

"They have to get in tune first. That's why it starts with breathing and meditation. These basic practices shut off the monkey brain. Shut off the chaos. Shut off the crazy, so you can listen. That's all I want people to do in the beginning. Just shut up. Turn everything off – and listen. That's where you start to connect with what YOU are feeling and not what your emotions are telling you to feel."

"Does traditional yoga training say the same thing, or is this Jason's spin on the training that he has done?"

"No, no, no, it's partially from my training but the whole point of yoga is to quiet the mind. That's it."

"I heard once that the point of yoga was to prepare the body for death, for the release of the spirit. Is that true?"

"Not in anything I've read." I laugh. "The most basic fundamental point of all the yoga I've studied is to quiet the mind so that you can connect to your True Self."

"Maybe part of the reason it's so successful in the West is because we've lost our own systematic ways of quieting the mind. We don't use anything from our Western tradition that allows us to do that anymore, except perhaps prayer."

"We have no ways, traditionally, to quiet the mind. And, now, we're stimulating ourselves more and more, on a more regular basis. If you go to the cinema everything is moving, flashing, you can't keep your eyes focused on one point for more than a fraction of a second. If you look at a film from the seventies or eighties though, everything seems slower. It's calmer and relaxing."

"Did you ever watch *Lassie* when you were a kid?" Sandra asks.

"Yes, yes."

"If you watch that now it's amazing. Only one thing

happens in half an hour!"

I laugh. "If that show were being made today, that half an hour would be crammed with a thousand things. Lassie would find a cocaine smuggler, there would be prostitution, gun fights, *Pow! Bang! Pow, Pow!!*

"So, no, we don't have that peace around us at all these days. We have to concentrate on creating it. A lot of that sense of peace is lost in yoga practice, as well. People see it as exercise, for the most part. Exercise that makes them feel better and, sure, for five minutes at the end of a lesson, you get a bit of quiet. That's the only time most people feel it.

"The whole point I'm trying to make is that within yoga, asana is only a small step in the process. You are *supposed* to go past that. That's why you see some of these swamis and gurus that aren't really in good shape. They don't need asana anymore. Their practice has shifted to a completely intellectual one. They are more consciously aware." I pause. "Maybe not all the time, all the way, but more so than asana can get you to.

"In yoga, it's called *The Eight Limbs*. The eight steps to reaching Samadhi, which is total focus of the mind. In that space you can start to truly destroy the ego, if you like."

"Which, in theory, you *can* achieve in life."

"Of course. Of course."

"So why do you think you chose yoga as a tool to get to where you've gotten to? There's nothing Indian in you. Did you grow up in a place that was very yoga-focused?"

I laugh. "No, more witch-focused."

"Witch-focused?" She laughs. "Why do you think yoga was the path for you?"

"I don't know, honestly. Looking back, I think it was because I liked those five minutes at the end. It was the only exercise that gave me that sort of result. After a while, I started feeling more things. Feeling my intuition and really listening.

"For the first year that I lived in San Francisco, I lived in a very creepy house. Things weren't going so well for me at the time. I had rented a room, sight unseen, after just a few emails and phone calls with the tenants. When I arrived it was like walking into a crack den. One of the guys was missing half of his teeth and dangled a big cigar in the gaps where his teeth used to be. The other couldn't make eye contact and was softly hitting himself. It took me a while to find a job and friends, so I started doing yoga from books every day. Literally, seven days a week, for a year, to escape. It was with that intensity of practice that things started to become more clear."

"Is there anything else you think might be interesting to share about the idea of choosing certain paths to enlightenment? Because in a way yoga is one path. Even starting with the breath, you could have done Tai Chi."

"Of course."

"Could you use running to get there?"

"You could. Of course you could, because the only

thing that gets you there in the end is focus and clear intent. That's it."

"And how do you get to a point of clear intent? If you come from a place of need, financial need, for example, growing up. You might focus on everything that you didn't have growing up. People move to acquisition for a good reason. For stability, security, fulfillment – but that, in itself, might not be it."

"It probably won't make you happy. And that's when you have to question yourself *Why did I do this? How did I get here?*"

"So there is a kind of happiness barometer that keeps you on track?"

I laugh. "Yes!"

"When you aren't happy or there is a growing feeling of discontent, something is going wrong. If you are focused, you'll know what needs attention pretty quickly. If you aren't focused, you need to come back to learning how to do it. If you have pure intent and good focus, things happen. But if your intent is unclear and/or you have no focus, you won't go anywhere towards manifesting what will make you happy."

"That's one of the reasons I didn't like *The Secret*. All they said was to think about what you want, make a dream board and everything will turn out the way you picture it. No! *You have to fucking act!* You have to act and keep acting – with clear intention and clear focus, over time. I really don't know how to say it any other way.

"When I'm thinking, when I'm really in a process of active thinking, it's like a straight line to what I want. That's how my thoughts work. I see them, visually. Like shining a light in a dark space – there's a straight line of focus. Your intent needs to be behind that. Completely!

"My intent was and is that I want to know the truth. My focus is that I'm going to shine this light on that truth and I'm going to keep going in that direction. I'm going to follow every cue along the way until I get there. *Nothing* is going to distract me – it's only going to help me.

"That also changes your vision, because as you keep your focus the universe will throw things at you to help you get there. The universe doesn't want to impede you. You're here to fucking fly! To have a good time. You get stuck because you identify with your body, your emotions and all the distractions you create to stay put."

Sandra pauses, thinking. "So why do people do that? Why would anyone choose to get caught up in all that drama and emotion instead of flying?"

"Fear. Fear of proper change. People don't like change.

"And people don't like doing nothing, so when they don't know what to do, they either chase things they know, or create emotional drama to distract them from what they don't know."

"You've said two things there that are pretty big and pretty interesting. One is that the universe wants you to fly. You've talked about a benevolent universe, in a way, as opposed to a completely neutral one."

"I'm speaking of that in the sense of energy, not in the sense of a being. The energy is moving and constant. The universe exists only inside of you and in the things you make of it. What I mean is that there is a beautiful flow to your life that is always there. You hinder the flow by being attached to the ego and doing its desires, instead of listening to your own."

"The other idea that came up was this idea that nobody is here to do nothing. Doing nothing is death."

"Doing nothing is boring. Why would consciousness want to be bored?"

Sandra frowns. "But creating an emotional drama is not doing *nothing.*"

"And that's okay. That's fine – as long as you are happy with it. If you're not happy then we have to figure out why you are doing what you are doing and change the activity. The whole point is to break people out of behavioral patterns when they realize and decide that behavior is not who they are or what they want to be."

"It comes back to the happiness question. Happiness is a kind of barometer. If you're not happy, something is not right."

"Exactly - so fix it!"

We laugh.

"If you're not happy in a country like this - with enough to eat, shelter, peace and people around you - then you have to ask *Why?* Only most people don't. Most of my students who take private coaching sessions don't return for more than two visits in a row because we shake things up so much. The coaching either needs time to settle and they need to process or the students go through a period of *Oh fuck, I wasn't ready for that! That's not really what I want! Or is it?* That's why I always start my coaching by asking, *Why are you here?* I want you to do what *you* want to do!"

Do this before you do anything

"Yoga is the settling of the mind into silence.
When the mind has settled, we are established into
our essential nature, which is unbounded consciousness.
Our essential nature is usually overshadowed
by the activity of the mind."
- *Patanjali, Yoga Sutras*

During these months of going through the awakening process, I wondered if I could set up a guide to help other people along the way. Was there a right order of steps to take that would apply to everyone wanting to open their eyes? And there is, kind of, at least with regards to how to start paying attention and beginning the process. If nothing else, I hope you take this with you from reading this book.

Breathe

I will say it again: everything begins with the breath. Doing this simple exercise daily will show you just how important correct breathing is.

Sit up straight and close your eyes. If you need a physical focal point for your diaphragm, place one hand above your navel and start breathing into that space. The idea is to take the breath from the chest and bring it down to the area between the rib cage and the navel. As you begin breathing towards your hand, you will feel a slight resistance from your diaphragm. This is because it is tight from not having been used properly. Breath into that space, into that resistance. Your diaphragm can be trained like any other muscle in your body. When you breathe in, try to expand the diaphragm down towards your waist. As you breath out, contract it up into your rib cage. The idea is to lengthen the breath and as you do that, to increase your oxygen supply.

Do this simple exercise for ten minutes as soon as you get out of bed in the morning and before you return to bed at night. It's a very simple exercise and a profound one. If you want to change something, anything, about your life, you must also change part of your routine.

Meditate

Once you've made a strong, conscious connection to your breath, you can make that connection stronger by turning this exercise into a proper meditation practice. Extend these ten minutes to fifteen minutes and see how much of a difference this can make. You will eventually be able to breathe very deeply, very naturally, long and slow.

Once you master that, practice maintaining focus. Isolate one part of your breath and focus your attention there. It can be the movement of the belly or the sensation of the air passing through your nostrils. Any time that you realize your mind has wandered and you are thinking about something other than your breath, catch yourself, take control and bring your focus back to the point of the breath that you were watching.

This exercise is simple, very effective and yet extremely difficult. It takes a lot of time to master. Repetition is key. You must teach the mind that you are in control and you do that by learning to keep your focus.

Listen

When you are able to maintain a state of clear focus - the mind, quiet and the breath, calm - you can begin to truly listen. Don't force anything. Watch. Observe. Listen. Feel.

If you try to force a response, your mind will take over. Then, you have to start over again with controlling your focus. This place of calm breath, quiet mind and openness is the place you want to sit in meditation. It's the place to get comfortable, where you can turn off the noise and really go inside. That's where you sense your True Self. That is Atman.

Cultivating this space will improve your overall wellbeing and contentment with life. Once you understand the concept and the process, try to come back to this space as often as you can. Habitually. If you are genuinely happy with the life you are living – in every sense of the word – then stop here and enjoy the new you.

However, if you want to go further, then let the games begin.

Be Aware

Now you can start to have fun with the universe as it stands within Maya. In this new found space of Atman, you want to increase your awareness of what's happening around you in your daily life.

Observe your life as you would your breath in the meditation and breathing practice. Look for things that catch your eye unexpectedly or jump right at you, out of the blue. Pay attention. When something surprises you or just seems different in a way that you can feel but not necessarily define, follow it! Like Alice following the white rabbit to Wonderland.

When you start looking you can actually see the patterns, the structure, the rhythms of universal energy and how it affects you and the world around you.

Once you can see it, once you know it is there, you can learn to communicate with it using words, intent and action. When you recognize this energy and respond to it, the universe answers. Maybe not immediately, but by communicating with it you set in motion the wheels of change.

This is where the concept of conscious co-creation comes from. By acting on cues from the universe, you let it know that you are paying attention and are ready and willing to follow. Life becomes a game, and you are both player and co-creator.

Question

Taking this playful state of heightened awareness into your daily life begin to question your life and the reality around you. This is where the death of the False Self begins.

If you are happy with your playful life within Maya, by all means, stay there. In order to go further, you will have to be very clear about the separation of the ego and must ask your questions from the silent space you have found through breathing and meditation.

So start asking your questions and listening / feeling / seeing for the answers. Sometimes the answers come quickly. Sometimes the answers take months. But the point is to stay focused on one! Stay focused on that one question until it has been understood or made irrelevant, and then move to the next one.

By doing this you slowly begin to tear away the pieces that make up the ego. One by one, you remove a part of yourself, a belief that no longer has meaning. Some of these removals are light, liberating epiphanies and others are painful and prolonged. It depends on the question you're working on at the time – and your investment in having the answer.

There is no right order of questions, you can start where you will. They all lead to the same answer in the end. Don't worry about what you are asking, just stay focused, and be willing to surrender to whatever comes up, regardless of what you think that might mean.

I share with you here, from my experience, the best way someone can start to wake up and take control of their lives. So think about what you really want when you begin this process. The world is literally what you make of it. Go make something amazing! Or, if you prefer, burn the house down! It's all up to you in the end.

Afterword

"And now, the end is near
And so I face the final curtain
My friend, I'll say it clear
I'll state my case, of which I'm certain

I've lived a life that's full
I've traveled each and every highway
But more, much more than this
I did it my way"

- Paul Anka, singer

I had two goals in mind in writing this book. First, I wanted to give you a glimpse of what the awakening process was like because I have never experienced anything like this in my 20 years as a yogi.

When all you have experienced is Maya and you start to step out of it, one can only expect it to be unlike anything else – and it most certainly is.

My life has totally changed, as have I – because I no longer exist. The self is dead. Now, I only exist as consciousness. The person that you know as Jason is still here because he has nowhere else to be. I am enjoying the show but my awareness is pure, clean and transparent. And, this is possible for any human.

Second, I wanted to share with you how I got here. I truly hope you have understood that no one can help you get here. You have to come check it out for yourself.

That might sound scary but the reality is that this is a solo mission. No teacher, guru, elder, priest, saint or savior can get you here. Those are all faces of Maya. They are distractions to take you off course.

Everything you want to know is sitting deep inside you. You just have to relinquish everything that you believe and let it all go. Destroy it, actually. The truth is buried underneath the layers of garbage, fear and conditioning that you have acquired throughout your life. Those things are not you and must be removed. Only after removing these layers will you get to the truth that's already there. See this process more as an unlearning, than a learning process.

If I could leave you with any advice it would be this: breathe, surrender to the flow, focus on what you really want and act when the universe gives you signs.

There is no such thing as a coincidence or deja vu. Those things that sparkle and get your attention, that's the language of the universe. Those are the things you need to follow. Shine the light there.

Of course, I'm writing this and I'm certainly no elder, priest, saint or savior. And everything I've said might be wrong. But, if reading this book has caused you to stop, for even a moment, and go back to your True Self and question your reality, then it's done its job. Reconnect to your True Self. See where you are and what you want. If your eyes and awareness stay open, the universe can take it from there.

Contact Information

To find out more about Jason and his yoga schools visit:
youcanyoga.nl

> You Can Yoga
> Stadionweg 283 & Aalsmeerweg 25
> Amsterdam
> The Netherlands
> info@youcanyoga.nl

Here you can learn about ongoing classes, intensive courses, retreats, workshops and other special events lead by Jason and the wonderfully diverse You Can Yoga staff of teachers and practitioners.

Acknowledgements

If you've made it this far, I'd like to thank you, the reader, for taking the time to read my story and hopefully reflecting on your own along the way. I'd also like to thank Gianuario Muntoni for taking care of me, who ever that is, while all of this was going down and to Sandra Guy for being such a pivotal part of the entire book writing process. Furthermore, I'd like to give a very special thank you to Tasha Shives, Erica Canon, Demian Rosenblatt and Kim Chandler McDonald for sharing their time and energy with the process. And thank you to the first round of readers for helping me find the best voice in which to share this experience.